# YESTERYEAR MEETS *today*

NANCY A CUSACK

# Dedication

*To my dad, Harold Cusack, who always thought I was smart, and looked at me like I was something special.*

# Contents

# Preface

My mom, Ruby M. Cusack, was a teacher, genealogist, book lover and storyteller. She loved to tell stories about her childhood, growing up on a farm in rural New Brunswick with her parents, four brothers, her grandparents, and extended family close by. She attended a one-room schoolhouse in Titusville, New Brunswick, where she later taught when she finished teachers' college at the age of 19.

From a very early age, I recall sitting for hours at my mom's dining room table, surrounded by her books, genealogy material, family albums and photographs as she would recount stories from her childhood. Tales of fishing in the Salt Springs Brook, haying in the summer, her Gramps' horses, and the one-room schoolhouse she attended, all describing a simpler way of life - hard work, family, resourcefulness, and community.

Ruby died in February 2022, leaving behind all her stories that often circulate in my thoughts. I want to honour my mom by sharing the stories she told me of Titusville in the 1940s. I have paired each story with a topic of interest, many of these issues involving mental health. I have been a licensed counselling therapist for many years and want to share my knowledge as well as my mother's stories, incorporating a look at mental health and what we all can learn from a time when life was perhaps simpler.

Ruby referred to the past as yesteryear, and her stories were of yesteryear. My work is from today, and includes information and knowledge of issues, topics and struggles that impact society today as well as in the 1940s, or as Ruby would say, yesteryear. There are issues we know more about today, most not new issues, but today we have words to describe them that didn't exist in the 1940s, words that put meaning and understanding to feelings, situations, and emotions. This book *Yesteryear Meets Today* combines nostalgia with issues and topics faced today and encountered in times gone by.

*Yesteryear Meets Today* is a book of short stories, each story containing four parts. There's a Ruby Piece, an educational piece, a book recommendation to honour Ruby's love of books, and an 'oh, by the way', a saying Ruby was known for. I hope you enjoy it, I certainly enjoyed putting it together and sharing my mom and her stories with the world.

# Acknowledgements

Thank you, Marina McCarron, obviously the most patient and efficient editor in the world.

InsideOut Press and Kim Olver's team were gracious and kind to me as I navigated the world as a new author. I appreciate the entire team.

Thanks to my friends who should have been photographers: Tammy Smith, Charlene Downey, and Elizabeth Crouchman, who provided photos for the front cover. My artist friend Deb Perry, who provided artwork, is creative, and totally gets me.

My husband, Patrick McMullon, who has always been smarter than me, but too humble to notice, and my lovely little children who are all grown up: Jack and Annie, thank you for being wonderful humans.

My many friends, who have helped me and encouraged me. Too many to mention, but here are a few: Patty Hoyt, Linda MacDonald, Rebecca Crouchman, and Lee Murphy Nobbs, who are more like sisters than friends. Shelley Scott who missed her calling as an editor. Ellen and Peter Murphy who were adored by my mother Ruby, and by me.

# The Moose Bird

*Ruby*

As we left school on that sunny March Day, we could hear the water dripping from the icicles on the eaves of our one-room schoolhouse. There was still snow on the ground and ice in the brook, but we could hear it cracking and the water flowing beneath the surface that grew softer with each passing day. The days were getting longer! Today the sun was bright, reflecting off the snow. In the distance, Clarence Campbell was tapping a maple tree; the sun and warmer temperatures encouraging the sap run, and Clarence would be turning his collection into maple syrup. Birds were singing and we could hear the flutter of their wings, especially the chickadees, as they moved from tree to tree along our country road. We saw nuthatches, juncos, and finches. Mum said to be on the lookout for the robins, as their return to New Brunswick was a sure sign of spring. We didn't see any blue jays, and I was happy about that, as their presence and call were a sign that rain was coming. I was most fond of the blue jays' relative, the moose bird, which seemed almost tame. Unlike the barn swallows that dive bombed my cat Ginger, the moose birds are sophisticated and cordial. Gramp always said that moose birds are the reincarnated spirits of old lumberjacks.

## Nancy

The Canada Jay, also known as the moose bird, gray jay, camp robber, whiskey jack and gorbey, is a relatively large songbird. These intelligent and inquisitive birds live across North America from northeastern Alaska to Newfoundland and Labrador. Their key habitat is coniferous trees in regions with colder temperatures. (Coniferous trees, also known as evergreen trees, grow needles instead of leaves and cones instead of flowers). Moose birds are easily tamed and act confident and secure around humans. They are monogamous, having one partner for life. They breed at two years of age, building a nest and laying eggs in a mature coniferous tree, most commonly a spruce. Nests are built on the southwest side of a tree for the sun's warmth. Moose birds have been seen landing on moose to remove and eat engorged ticks. A symbiotic relationship for sure, providing food for the bird while removing the nasty parasite from the moose. Researchers have found large ticks in moose birds' nests with their hatchlings. It is hypothesized that these engorged ticks were too big to be eaten, so were used as 'hot water bottles' to keep the hatchlings warm when their mother was not in the nest.

Moose birds survive in the harsh Canadian winter by storing their food when it is plentiful under the bark of trees. This stored food, known as a cache, provides nourishment when food is scarce at the end of winter. The birds are opportunistic scavengers, and their diet generally consists of insects, berries, meat, and vegetables. Food intended for storage is manipulated in their mouth and coated with sticky saliva, which makes it adhere to anything it touches. A single moose bird can hide thousands of pieces of food every year and then recover it from memory months later.

In the last few years, woodsmen and those who frequent the forests in New Brunswick have reported a decline in moose bird sightings. It is speculated that their cache is rotting due to warmer temperatures and the jays are starving. Moose birds associate humans with food. They have been known to approach humans for treats and to steal unattended food from camps or from woodsmen eating their lunch. Superstition in New Brunswick says moose birds may be the souls of dead lumberjacks. Another superstition held is how woodsmen would not harm the moose bird, believing that whatever they inflicted on the bird would happen to them. Folklore has circulated in New Brunswick about a man who plucked all a moose bird's feathers and woke the next morning having lost all his hair.

Might moose birds really be reincarnated lumberjacks? I'm not sure, but they are fun to watch, and when their brown eyes look right into yours, it is easy to think *maybe, just maybe*.

*The Secret Life of Birds* is a children's book by Moira Butterfield. This collection of stories and bird facts about our feathered friends includes beautiful folklore stories of birds all around the world.

Oh, by the way, it's never too soon to teach children about nature and the beauty all around them. It's also a good reminder for adults that watching and feeding the birds can be therapeutic and helps us slow down and appreciate the simple, beautiful things in life.

# Neurodiversity

## Ruby

When other boys were in the woods with their rifles hunting for squirrels, or roughhousing with other boys, my little brother Cliff was reading music, helping Mum make a Washington pie, or showing me how fast he could crochet a granny square for the afghan Gram was making. Cliff could sing and play the piano. He was naturally, effortlessly musical and because of this gift he was instantly drawn to the choir at church. Everything seemed to come so easy to him. Cliff was also a dedicated animal lover like me.

## Nancy

Today, our young Cliff would be known as gifted. Gifted children are children who have an exceptional talent or natural ability. Giftedness is a form of neurodiversity. Neurodiversity is a term that has entered the vernacular of today. The word is used to describe the plethora of differences in how people's brains behave. Neurodivergent people have distinctly different strengths and challenges compared to those who are neurotypical. In the past, terms *normal* and *weird* were regularly used in place of *neurotypical* and *neurodiverse*. Previously, in the not-so-distant past, society was more rigid, and many held the belief that people were either normal or weird. Boys who liked trucks were *normal* while boys who liked to bake were *weird*. Girls who liked dolls were *normal*, however girls who liked to play in the mud were *weird*. At one time students who wrote with their left hand were, best-case scenario, reprimanded, worst-case scenario, *strapped* with the terror-provoking leather strap for refusing to hold a pencil 'the normal way' with the right hand.

We know so much more about the functioning of the brain today than we did in the 1940s. We know that some people are left-handed. We understand, without hesitation, that there is absolutely nothing wrong with individuals who use their left hand, their brains simply work differently. This difference results in left hand dominance, something unique considering that 88% of the population is right-handed.

Some people are naturally musical or creative. Some can memorize information easily, while others are able to repair anything or construct anything. Some people can navigate through the woods easily without a compass, and some can perform mathematical equations instantly in their head.

With knowledge and understanding regarding the differences and complexity of the human brain and neurodiversity, our education system and our society can change how neurodiverse children are treated. Instead of viewing neurodiverse children as *abnormal,* with a mission to transform them to *typical,* parents, teachers, and others in the education sector can build on strengths and their natural, creative, and sometimes gifted, capabilities or *superpowers.* Neurodiverse children can be encouraged to accept themselves and develop strategies to view, and interact with their world with confidence, pride, and purpose.

My grandparents (Ruby's parents) were ahead of their time. They understood and appreciated the individual strengths and challenges of each of their five children. They guided each of their children toward a life and career where they could thrive. My uncle Cliff is a gifted singer and piano player and had a successful career in the banking industry. He was encouraged to be himself and he flourished.

*Midnight and Moon* is a children's picture book written by local author Kelly Cooper. This delightful book tells the story of a young girl named Clara, who doesn't speak, and Moon, a blind horse, who, like Clara, struggles to find his 'place' in the world. It is a wonderful children's book about neurodiversity and friendship.

Oh, by the way, the author of this book, Kelly Cooper, lives on a farm in rural New Brunswick, is a teacher and loves books, just like my mom Ruby.

# Cramp Nuts

*Ruby*

I woke in the middle of the night to the sound of Mum moaning and pacing in her bedroom. This was not the first time I had heard this in the night. I could hear Dad talking, so tiptoed down the hall to their room. Dad turned just as I was entering the room and sternly told me to get back to bed. Dad spoke gruffly to me most times and this time was no different. He pointed in the direction of my bedroom. I was reluctantly returning to my room when I heard mom say, 'Art, I know how to fix this once and for all'. It was good to hear her voice and she sounded confident, which made me worry less about her. I fell back to sleep quickly curling up with my cat Ginger.

The next morning Mum was in the kitchen. She was always in the kitchen. I could see Dad in the back porch putting on his coat and hat and reaching for the saw. Mom called to him, 'Art, Ruby is up. Take her with you and don't be so gruff with her, she's just a little girl.' Mum would always speak softly to me and was not afraid to let Dad know when he was being a bit too stern with me. I put on my warm coat and boots, and we set off down the path, past the barn, along the brook and into the woods.

The ground below my boots was crunching with every step I took. It was early November, and I could see my breath, could feel the cool air entering my lungs on this frosty morning. Dad and I were on a hunt, a special hunt for Mum. She was having terrible leg cramps at night and had sent us to find a cramp nut. Dad explained that a cramp nut could be found on a maple tree, but not all maple trees had them. It didn't take long before we spotted a tree that had several bulges on it. Dad used the axe to cut a branch off that had one of these bulges. The branch was about two feet long and the bump was the size of a rolled-up pair of wool socks. Dad pointed at the lumpy thing and said, 'See that? That's a cramp nut, just what we are looking for.'

When we arrived back home, Dad excitedly announced, 'Mae, we found one'. Mum was glad to see us and took the cramp nut branch upstairs, putting it under her bed. She announced there would be no more leg cramps now that she had a cramp nut under her bed. Low and behold, she was right, and I was never awakened in the night again to Mum's agony.

*Nancy:*

Today we call cramp nuts tree burls, and artisans often make beautiful bowls from them. They are large knot-like projections on tree trunks and sometimes branches. Why these abnormal tree growths occur is unknown, but it is suspected a fungus, virus, or parasite causes this irregular formation.

How do these tree growths treat leg cramps? Well, there is no evidence to support that they do. It's a bit of a mystery…or is it?

Leg cramps are painful and sudden involuntary muscle contractions and can last seconds or several minutes. They usually happen in the calf of the leg but can also occur in the foot, hamstring, or thigh. They are sometimes referred to as a Charley horse. They are not harmful but do cause significant discomfort.

Leg cramps are more common with age and more prominent in females. The Medical University of South Carolina Health (http://www.muschealth.org) suggest sixty percent of adults experience leg cramps. They are reported to happen seventy-five percent of the time at night and are called idiopathic cramps, meaning a cramp with unknown cause.

There are speculations that these leg cramps may be caused by the following:

1. Sitting or standing for long periods of time. Stretching is the recommended treatment if this is the cause.
2. A nutrient deficiency such as a lack of magnesium, calcium and/ or potassium. Eating foods rich in these nutrients is suggested by doctors. Food high in magnesium, potassium and calcium includes bananas, avocados, and sweet potatoes.
3. Dehydration: Increasing water intake and limiting alcohol and caffeine may help.
4. Changing of seasons: managing the discomfort when cramps occur by using ice/heat, standing, walking, stretching, and massaging the area.

One explanation of why the cramp nut treats these painful sensations is the placebo effect.

The placebo effect refers to a positive outcome, health improving, and symptoms being alleviated after using a treatment that has no therapeutic value or benefit. Placebos can impact how individuals perceive their condition, encouraging the body to relieve symptoms, which in turn demonstrates the role the brain plays on physical health. In essence the placebo effect is a belief treatment will work. This belief causes a strong connection between how the brain and body work together, causing an individual to experience less pain and create a positive outcome.

There are two main hypotheses on how placebos work:

1. Response expectation is a belief that the placebo will help the pain, which leads the person to feel better. They expect to feel better, therefore they do. This is a lot like positive thinking. When you think positively, the likelihood of a positive outcome increases.

2. Classical conditioning occurs when an active treatment is being used at the same time as the placebo and the brain makes the association that the placebo is what is alleviating the symptoms. For example, if the leg cramps are caused by lack of potassium, but the individual also starts eating more bananas while the cramp nut is under the bed, the brain makes the association that the cramp nut is alleviating the pain when it may be the bananas.

There is also an effect opposite to the placebo effect called the nocebo effect. In this case when a negative outcome happens the individual believes a proven intervention will cause harm. For example, the individual starts taking a medication and they are convinced they will have all the side effects of the medication, making them feel worse rather than better. This is a lot like negative thinking, where thinking negatively may cause the likelihood of negative outcomes to increase.

The placebo and the nocebo effect demonstrate how powerful our thoughts can be. If we can change our thoughts, we can change our outlook and our behaviours, and ultimately change the way we feel.

Oh, by the way, if you are interested in turning cramp nuts into bowls, Richard Raffan has a great book called *The Art of Turned Bowls*. Richard has been a successful and skilled artisan in wood turning since 1970. In this book, he shares his skill, techniques, and passion for his craft with others. He includes many beautiful illustrations and tips on how to create and design your own turned bowls.

*Photo credit to Jacqueline Carr*

# Shivaree

*Ruby*

Cliff was rummaging behind the flour barrel in the pantry in search of the water dipper. I had already laid claim to two pots and Ken had their lids. Mum had Flossie the cow's bell, and Dad had an old accordion. Our teacher, Miss Smith, had married Bud Titus this afternoon, and tomorrow they would be heading away on their honeymoon. Tonight though, they would be surprised by a Shivaree.

At dark the whole community would show up outside their house making a ruckus until they were all invited in for tea and sweets. Newlyweds in the country generally tried to keep their whereabouts secret on the night they got hitched, and with good reason. Community members made it their mission to find out where they would be and interrupt any newlywed 'activities'. As we quietly walked to their place just up the road, neighbours joined us as we passed their houses. It was a beautiful night in September, the stars were shining, and the moon was a small crescent high in the night sky. We quietly arrived at the Titus farm and waited. Shortly after our arrival, the lights went out. We waited a couple of minutes longer, and then the silence was broken by Dad's attempt at playing the accordion. That was our cue to join in. We banged on pots, pans, metal lids and some men even fired their shotguns. Some of the women sang as loud as they could. It wasn't long before the front door opened. We all cheered and clapped for the newly married couple. I could see that Miss Smith was embarrassed in her housecoat as she ushered us all in for tea.

## Nancy

A shivaree is a noisy serenade performed by a group of people to celebrate a marriage. Wedding guests show up uninvited to the home of the newlyweds, create a ruckus, and 'force' entry into the home. Communities viewed a shivaree as the first ordeal for a married couple to tackle together, somewhat of a hazing to welcome the newly married couple into the community of other married couples. A shivaree was an activity of celebration that brought the community together to participate in a bit of mischief, good faith, and clean fun.

This noisy social event is the first big surprise the couple must navigate. How will they manage this mob who has interrupted their first big night together? How will they handle this? What decisions do they need to make together? This is a common question that married couples often face: How do we deal with this together? And 'this' can take many forms throughout a marriage, whether it's a decision about having children, raising children, or how to manage finances. Married couples are always making decisions together which can easily lead to conflict when a couple has opposing opinions or views on issues.

There have been tons of books written on how to be happy in a marriage. There is so much information on the internet about this topic that it can certainly become overwhelming. I'm going to share with you a few principles of marriage that are basic, yet important.

Decision-making and communication are the threads that hold most things together in a marriage. How a couple communicates and how a couple makes decisions can be the glue that holds everything together when issues arise. All the issues in life that will arise can be more easily handled when a couple communicates and makes decisions in a way that works for both individuals. Below are some practical things to consider about decision-making and communication:

1. Know yourself. Love yourself, express yourself, and communicate to your partner who you are, what you like, what hobbies you enjoy, and what qualities you like in other people. Be authentic, honest, and kind. Only you can control what you say, how you say it, and how you behave.

2. Be kind. This does not mean having to be positive, agreeable, and sweet all the time, it means speaking your mind in a kind manner. Have boundaries and speak up when you need to. Disagreeing does not mean conflict, but can facilitate negotiation, compromise, and suitable outcomes.

3. Know that arguments are normal and should always have a resolution. Do not walk away in the middle of an argument only to return like nothing happened. Arguments are required to change and grow as a couple. Make sure you listen and are respectful during an argument or disagreement. Make sure you find a solution through negotiation and reflect when it's over to make sure you both understand the outcome of the disagreement and the plan for moving forward.

4. Have a life outside of your marriage. Your partner does not have to be your best friend. You can both enjoy different activities and hobbies without the other. Have good friends that you can spend time with.

5. Acknowledge and accept who you married, who they are, and what they like to do. Do not attempt to change them or control them. If your spouse likes to paint and you don't, that's okay. Support their interest and encourage them to engage in this activity often.

6. Have boundaries. Express your needs, communicate what you want, and what you expect.

7. Remember you have needs as an individual and as a couple. As an individual you need connection, meaning, freedom, fun, a sense of power, and safety. As a couple you need the same. How we meet these needs may be different, and that's okay.

Your behaviour and words matter. Some behaviours will increase connection, while others will destroy the relationship. Dr William Glasser developed Choice Theory® and has written many books and promoted his theory on internal control to help couples navigate relationships through awareness of good and bad habits couples' practice. The habits below are from Dr Glasser's teachings:

The following behaviours will destroy relationships:

1. Criticizing – speaking negatively to your partner, using harsh

words like stupid and dumb, pointing out their faults, judging their appearance, and speaking in a disapproving manner.

2. Blaming – assigning responsibility for something bad happening, like saying, 'This is all your fault.'

3. Complaining – repeated expression of dissatisfaction, annoyance, and resentment with no resolution, usually with issues that one has no control over, such as the weather or other people's behaviour.

4. Nagging – constantly harassing, asking, or telling someone to do something.

5. Threatening – purposely expressing or suggesting harm causing another to feel frightened or vulnerable.

6. Punishing – making another suffer because of a belief they did something wrong or deserve a harsh consequence.

7. Bribing or rewarding to control – giving something, even affection, only to persuade a person to do something. Providing attention only to get something in return.

Note how the above habits are all action words. They are behaviours, and behaviours can be changed. Becoming aware of these toxic habits is the first step toward changing these behaviours.

The following are healthy habits and behaviours that strengthen relationships and foster connection:

1. Supporting - holding each other up in good times and bad, being loyal in word and deed, and believing in each other's dreams. Wanting each other to succeed and celebrating each other's success.

2. Encouraging - giving positivity and hope for future success.

3. Listening - making an effort to hear and understand, paying attention to another's words, providing feedback without judgement and acknowledging you hear each other.

4. Accepting - believing in each other and willingly deciding that your loved one is good enough just as they are.

5. Trusting - relying and depending on each other and having confidence and belief in one another's honesty and sincerity. Faith that the other does not have malicious intent.

6. Respecting - holding each other in high regard or esteem. Recognizing another's abilities and worth.

7. Negotiating differences - conferring with each other to come to terms or reach an agreement. Discussion with a purpose to resolve, which may warrant compromise from each party.

Knowledge and awareness are powerful as both help with understanding, growth and communication within a relationship.

My wonderful friend and colleague Kim Olver has written a

great book called *Secrets of Happy Couples: Loving Yourself, Your Partner and Your Life*. Kim's book empowers readers to focus on the things they can change within a relationship. Kim is also one of many who believe and promote Dr. Glasser's concepts to help couples live happier lives.

Oh, by the way, I've been with the same fella for over 30 years, and my mom, Ruby, was with my dad, Harold, for over 60 years! I have included our wedding pictures below.

# Community

*Ruby*

The snow had fallen steadily through the night and was piled as high as the top fence rail by sunrise. Cliff was finishing up his porridge when I entered the toasty warm kitchen. Mum was already fast at work with the wood range, providing the nicest heat for me, and the baking Mum was doing on this snowy Sunday morning. Today was a special day. Cliff would be playing the organ at the church. He was the best singer in the choir, in my opinion, and today he would be singing and playing the organ. He had been practicing all the hymns. My favorite was In the Garden, and that was the song he was playing today. Cliff had all the musical talent in our family. I could barely whistle and couldn't carry a tune even in a basket! Dad went to the church early to get the fire started, shovel a path, and to light the oil lamps, while Mum was making a pan of biscuits and date squares. Cliff and I would sneak a date square or two before leaving for church. The congregation would be invited back to our place after the service. Gram and Gramp would be there to support Cliff. The twins Ethel and Elsie, Sadie, and even my aunt Tillie would be there. It was going to be a real community affair.

*Nancy*

Community is defined as a group of people with a common characteristic or interest, living together within a larger society.

It is familiar and brings people together and provides support to each member. Community is a social unit with commonality such as location (living near one another), norms (unwritten rules that define behaviour or actions such as going to church every Sunday), religion (shared faith and religious beliefs), customs (traditions), and values (morals and beliefs that guide behaviour).

A community can provide purpose, meaning, connection, support, and fun. The term 'a sense of community' refers to a feeling of belonging, and a feeling that members matter, and everyone's needs are important and will be supported.

Being part of a group or community where one feels heard, supported and important provides a stronger sense of self and can help one cope with negative experiences and emotions. Community helps us be part of something bigger than just our individual self.

As humans we crave meaningful connections and a sense of belonging. We may not all love large groups, but we are wired for social connection. When people come together amazing things can happen.

The primary concept of psychiatrist, Dr.Glasser's choice theory is a simple yet very important principle – Glasser believed that many mental health issues are the result of a lack of meaningful connections and a lack of community. He studied and researched this theory and treated many patients struggling to be mentally well. He was a doctor and could easily prescribe medications, but he usually started first by teaching his patients what their basic human needs were and how to meet those needs. He rarely prescribed medications for mental health issues, considering himself more of a teacher, showing people how to meet their needs, knowing when these needs are met, they could start to feel joy again.

Dr. Glasser believed all humans have five basic needs. The first one is safety, and if we are not safe, the other needs don't really matter, as we are in a constant state of survival, searching for food, shelter, and safety. Most people today have a roof over their head and access to food, water, and shelter. Once this need is met the other needs move to the forefront. The second need is for connection, to have a sense of love and belonging. The third is for freedom and a sense that we have options. The fourth is having power and a sense that we are significant and have something to offer. The fifth one is my personal favorite: fun. The ability to play and engage in activities that we love is essential for happiness and fulfillment.

Once we know these needs, we can do what Glasser calls a Needs Profile to determine how we are doing and assess which needs are being met, and which one(s) are not. Being aware of our needs and our needs profile can show us what is lacking in our life and put us on a path to better fulfilling our needs, which in turn helps us live richer, happier lives. It can be simple to meet all the four needs by engaging in one activity, for example being connected in the community by attending the Baptist church and singing in the choir can foster a sense of connection and belonging. It may also be fun and give a sense of power and freedom.

Connection also refers to connection with the self. Each person may find different activities fun, so its important to know yourself and what you want. Some people love basketball, playing basketball, watching basketball, fundraising for basketball, and when engaging in these activities it is more likely that they will make meaningful connections with others that also enjoy basketball. Other people may enjoy sewing, quilting, making costumes and while engaging in these activities they will likely find their people and community, along with a sense of power, freedom and fun. Glasser pointed out that often one activity can meet all your needs. He also said its important to meet all your needs every day to maintain good mental health.

Today there are less people attending church, and I can't help but wonder if this is why more people seem to be struggling with their mental health. They've lost a sense of community which the church historically provided for its members.

One of Dr Glasser's first books, Choice Theory, discusses his theory and application in more detail. He includes in this book the principles and concepts of his theory and how to apply them individually, in communities and in organizations. It's an easy read that offers simple changes the reader can make to feel happier. Dr. Glasser believed that if behaviours and thoughts change, feelings will also change. How we feel about the self, others, and the environment will change if thinking and behaviours are changed.

Oh, by the way, Dr William Glasser lived in California but delivered his theory all over the world, establishing the William Glasser Institute, which continues to promote healthy people and healthy communities all over the world.

*Photo credit to Elizabeth Crouchman*

# Quilting

*Ruby*

I awoke to giant snow flurries falling past my bedroom window, snug as a bug in my feather tick bed, wrapped in a quilt Gram had made. It was early December, and there was not enough snow to go tobogganing. As I lay there wondering what the day may bring, I heard voices beneath me in the kitchen. The stove pipe ran through my bedroom so I could hear each time a stick of wood was placed in the stove, and conveniently, everyone's conversations. I loved listening to the grown-ups talk, getting caught up on all the gossip. I heard Dad come in and put kindling in the wood box and leave again. The voices were all women.

Curiosity got the best of me when I heard Gram's voice amongst the others. Downstairs I went to see what was going on. The kitchen was warm, as always, and smelled like bread and fresh firewood. Mum and Gram along with Mrs. Kilpatrick, Mrs. Baird, Mrs. Wagner, and Mrs. Morrison were all sitting around a large structure with wooden rails holding a big piece of material tight as they all sewed away, making small talk, and drinking tea. I quietly sat by the stove eavesdropping as the ladies quilted. I observed all the tiny pieces of fabric that were used, the shiny thimbles on each of their hands, the precision of their stitches, and their laughter. It seemed like something much bigger was going on besides a quilting bee in our kitchen.

## Nancy

A quilting bee is a social gathering during which a quilt is made. The word bee in this context is derived from a prayer or favour and refers to forms of communal work that benefit a neighbour. In the 1940s, quilting and quilting bees were a cheap hobby that utilized small pieces of leftover fabric. These bits of material were sewn together to form patterns within squares, and the squares were then sewn together to form a large quilt top. In some quilting bees, each individual quilter would design their own section of the quilt, and then each section would be carefully sewed together, representing the creativity of each quilter.

The definition of quilting is a specific type of sewing that includes attaching three layers of fabric that include the quilt top, the back, and the batting which is insulating and provides the warmth. Once the top is completed, the batting is sandwiched between the top and back, the entire three layers are squared up and pulled taut on wooden quilt rails, and then sewn, or quilted, with a design. The final quilting design can be as simple as straight lines to more complex designs of flowers or even birds.

Today quilting is typically done by machine and the designs of the stitching are all programmed and executed by computer software technology. In the 1940s though, it was all done by hand and took a very long time to complete, which is why many women would get together to work on a quilt. As the old saying goes, 'many hands make light work'. This expression spotlights the importance of combined effort, and how a tough task can be less demanding when multiple people help.

Quilting not only creates beauty and comfort from left over fabric but can also be very good for mental health and well-being. It gives the creator a sense of accomplishment, and this sense is a human need that is uplifting. Quilting requires planning, problem solving, design and execution, which improves cognitive functioning and increases the ability to think critically. The process of quilting requires spatial thinking, creative thinking, and lights up the social engagement parts of the brain when individuals gather to quilt. Quilting increases hand eye coordination and motor skill functioning, improves focus, concentration, provides purpose, meaning, a sense of significance and can even improve sleep. Quilting is also an activity that can relieve stress and anxiety. Many quilters report a 'flow' that happens when they are totally absorbed in their work and in the zone. Blocking out the entire world while working on their project enhances rhythm and calm. This type of flow provides a break from everyday worries and fosters relaxation. Today's word for activities that do this is mindfulness, which means in the moment, being present, and only thinking and focusing on the here and now, not the past or future.

Quilting can provide connection to others who also enjoy the hobby, which can build a sense of community. Choosing fabric, colours, and designs fosters a sense of freedom and autonomy in each quilter, nurturing creativity, and providing a space for artistic talent. Creating something beautiful feels good. Working with bright colours can boost one's mood, is satisfying to the eye, and uplifts the spirit. It is also fun, and fun is something we all need in our lives.

A finished quilt represents warmth, comfort, expression,

and is a reminder that women overcome hardship by coming together and helping one another, being creative and patient together.

Good friends are like quilts: they age with you, yet never lose their warmth.

Cleo Lampos is a retired teacher and the author of a cheerful book called *Creating Comfort-ers,* independently published in 2021. Cleo spent a lifetime surrounded by rural quilters. Her book includes the history and philosophy of quilting along with stories of grace and love that every quilter gives to turn fabric into beauty, comfort, hope and cheer. Her book also includes a colorful showcase of completed quilts.

Oh, by the way, most communities have the sweetest little quilt shops where experienced quilters teach the art and skill of quilting, while helping you with design and fabric selection. In my community there are at least 4 that I know of, however I didn't know they existed until I became interested in quilting. A quick Google or Facebook search may help you find these local gems where women, and even some men, gather to shop, design, and create with one another.

*Photo credit to Charlene Downey*

*Photo credit to Elizabeth Crouchman*

# Adder Tongues

*Ruby*

As Cliff and I meandered home from school, we took a short cut through the meadow alongside the brook. The ground beneath our feet was very damp and made a slurping sound with every step we took. Cliff was eying the brook, looking for fish and anticipating fishing season. I was looking for flowers along the bank, remembering how we had picked them last year. I couldn't quite remember their name, but they were a sure sign of spring and gave us hope that summer was just around the corner. We sloshed away in the meadow, and I was thankful Mum told us to wear our gum rubber boots to school. Cliff saw them first - delicate yellow flowers atop a thin green stalk with two spotted green leaves at their base. I got right to work picking a bunch for Mum, hoping this would make her less annoyed at the mud that covered our boots and pant legs.

I was careful with my bouquet as we made our way home. When we entered the kitchen, the smell of ham and corn scallop filled the room. Ken was completing his lessons at the kitchen table. I presented the flowers to Mum announcing these were the first flowers of spring, and at that moment their name came to me: ADDER TONGUES. That's what they were called. I was quite proud of myself for my knowledge when Ken spoke up and said, 'They are called adder's tongue not adder tongues'. I had switched up where the 's' belonged. Ken was always right and knew everything about everything. As I stood in the kitchen by the warmth of the wood range, I didn't care what they were called, because they were a sure sign of warmer days ahead - days of swimming in the brook, catching fish, and church picnics.

*Nancy*

Adder's tongue is one of the first flowers to bloom in early spring, even before the surrounding trees leaf out. They are a type of lily, also known as dog tooth violet, trout lily and fawn lily. The Wildlife Trust (http//www.muschealth.org) reports they grow in damp woodlands and often can be found alongside a stream or brook as they prefer moist soil. It is a single yellow flower with six petals atop a thin stalk with two leaves at the base. The flower closes at night and opens again in the daylight. The name adder's tongue is in reference to the tongue like shape of the flowering shoot as it rises in early spring and resembles the open mouth of a snake. This dainty little wildflower is a sign of warmer days, and a reminder that summer is just around the corner.

Hope is an optimistic view and belief that the future will be better and brighter days are ahead. It can apply to one's life or the world in general. Having hope is important for good mental health. Hope improves our quality of life, reduces stress, and increases joy and happiness. It ushers in peace, confidence and purpose while enhancing our strength to face challenges in our lives.

Hope creates energy and passion, encourages us to dream of the future, fosters solution focused and goal-oriented thoughts, the development of strategies to achieve goals and provides motivation for follow through. When we have hope we engage more with others, and with activities we love that provide a sense of accomplishment.

Hope leads to empathy, understanding and kindness. These three skills foster health, happiness, and connection.

Without hope, one can become lonely, disengaged, and disconnected from family, friends, and the world. Lack of hope is associated with depression and anxiety.

Practical strategies to develop or increase hope:

1. Acknowledge your accomplishments. Write them down.
2. Take care of yourself. You don't have to follow a strict diet or run a marathon but drink some water, eat some nutritious food, move your body, spend some time in nature, and get some sleep.
3. Have fun by engaging in activities and hobbies you enjoy.
4. Build relationships that are supportive and caring. Nurture friendships with common interests that encourage you and help you feel good.
5. Look around, appreciate what you have, and slow down.

Today there is a modern saying to 'look for glimmers' meaning glimmers of hope. These glimmers are all around and if we look around for them, they will be found. Be aware of your surroundings, pay attention, and notice. Notice nature, try to catch others being kind, notice patterns that may exist on rocks, on trees, or even in the snow. Finding colourful sea glass on the beach or finding a heart shaped rock can be examples. You may notice pretty patterns in the clouds, the smell of roses, or a colourful bird in your backyard. These are glimmers of hope. There is beauty, wonder and even miracles all around us. If you slow down and look around, you will see them.

Oh, by the way, hope is contagious. Once we have hope we start encouraging others, smiling, helping, and extending kindness. This behaviour encourages others to smile and be kind and have hope for brighter times ahead.

*Noticing* is a colorful, sweetly illustrated book for all ages, written by Kobi Yamada and illustrated by Elise Hurst. It is a story about noticing the little things, big things, and hidden things; a book that encourages the reader to observe their surroundings, make new discoveries and see the magic all around.

*Photo credit to Betty Ann Ryan*

# The Indian Devil

*Ruby*

It was a sunny summer morning as I walked into the kitchen. I could smell, before I could see, that Mum was baking. She asked me if I could help her make a Washington pie for the church picnic on Sunday. I despised cooking or anything to do with a kitchen really, so I quickly reminded Mum that Gramp needed my help in his potato field. I made my way to Gramps, walking along the pasture by the brook. I could see the horses Nell and Dan swishing their tails to keep the flies at bay. Gramp was already hard at work when I arrived. He handed me two flat rocks, gave me a wink and with a smile said, 'Get to work'.

The potato bugs were particularly bad that year, and they loved potato plant leaves as much as I loved Gram's potato scallop. It was my job to inspect each plant and squash each bug I found between the two rocks Gramp had provided. We were both working away in the heat when I noticed Nell and Dan were agitated, tossing their heads back and forth and pacing along the fence. Gramp noticed them too and had a slight look of concern on his face. Suddenly there was a terrifying screech. It sounded like a woman screaming and a baby crying. I froze, I couldn't move or even breathe. My hands were sweaty, and I felt tingly all over. I'd never felt so frightened. Gramp pointed up near the ridge on Stover Baird's property. There it was: a large Indian devil sitting on a rock. It sat there looking down at us for a few seconds before it turned and headed back up toward the tree line, and thankfully away from us. Gramp gave my shoulder a little squeeze and with a caring, kind look in his eyes said, 'He gave you quite a fright!'.

*Nancy*

The Indian devil is also known as the eastern panther, mountain lion, or cougar. It is a large cat with a very long tail and can weigh between 90-120 pounds. It is believed that only the females screech this terrifying sound in attempts to call a mate. Reported to have been extinct in New Brunswick since the 1930s, many sightings were reported in the 1940s and 50s. Today with the accurate sightings from high resolution trail cams, collection of fur samples, analysis of scat and paw prints along with DNA technology, it is evident that the eastern panther or Indian devil is certainly here in New Brunswick. According to Parks Canada (http://www.parks.canada.ca) researchers near Fundy National Park have solid evidence at two test sites that confirm their existence. The question now is how many are there and where they come from.

Seeing or hearing the screech of these elegant creatures can give you a fright! This is the brain's response to danger.

There is a part of the brain called the amygdala. The amygdala's job is to keep us safe and alerts us when danger is present. When the amygdala detects danger, it releases stress hormones that prepare the body to flee or fight the danger. There is often a freeze response that is instinctual while the body is preparing to run. This feels like an inability to move or speak, and a tingly feeling as adrenaline is being released into the body. When the brain senses danger, it shuts off the digestive system and the executive functioning centre. The executive functioning centre is responsible for thinking, analysis, speech, concentration, and problem solving. The brain knows the priority at that moment is safety, and there is no need to analyse information, have a conversation, or snack in the face of danger. The amygdala sends a boost of adrenaline directly to the muscles, in preparation to run or fight.

Once the threat is over (in my mum's case the cougar returned to the woods) the amygdala sends a message that it's okay to carry on, the threat is over.

In some instances, the amygdala becomes super sensitive after experiencing a stressful event. Instead of relaxing and calming down, the amygdala becomes overprotective, sending our body the message that there is danger when there is no apparent threat. The brain may make an association to the stressful event. An oversensitive amygdala remembers the danger and makes an association that other things are dangerous too that were present when the danger was detected. For example, the oversensitive amygdala can make an association that a potato field is dangerous along with the cougar that was present, which may cause the amygdala to send messages that there is danger in the form of stress hormones and adrenaline when there is no threat. The brain is remembering the danger that happened in the potato field and may make the association that potato fields are dangerous. Today this hypersensitive brain is referred to as an amygdala hijack.

Typically, after a scary event our body and brain recover quite quickly, and we can know and feel that the threat is over. Our executive functioning (ability to analyse, problem solve, have conversations) returns, our digestion is turned back on, and we can breathe normally again. If symptoms linger, or appear when there is no danger, meaning we feel like there is danger when there is not (hypervigilant) the amygdala may be working overtime, sending messages of danger to keep us safe. If this happens there is a calming strategy that can help the brain and nervous system to settle down, assuring the amygdala it's okay, the threat is over. This calming strategy is BREATHING. When there is danger, breathing will be impacted as the body prepares to fight or flee. When the threat has passed, or there is no danger anymore, focus on breathing in and breathing out. The outbreath stimulates the parasympathetic nervous system which activates relaxation. Just breathe.

Be mindful of what the built-in responsibility of the amygdala is - to keep us safe from danger. It will always fire when there is danger and activate the flight or fight response. That's what keeps us safe.

Oh, by the way, if you happen to be fortunate enough to see an eastern panther in its natural habitat, consider yourself lucky - they are a symbol of strength, leadership, and courage.

Peter Levine in his book *Waking the Tiger* normalizes the flight or fight response and gives more detail on this instinctual reaction in humans and other animals. He also provides strategies on how to recover from trauma when the fight or flight response is not turned off after a stressful or series of stressful events.

*Painting by artist Deb Perry*

*Photo credit to Tammy Smith*

# Hoarding

*Ruby*

Mum never considered herself a packrat, in her opinion she was simply saving things until they were needed. Glass jars were saved for pickling, string was rolled up, and paper bags folded. Gram was the same, she kept all my aunts' old clothes. My aunt Ethel was an identical twin to Elsie. They both were teachers with a flair for fashion. One day when Mum and I were visiting, Gram had one of Ethel's tweed blazars in her lap in the parlour. The blazer was well used and frayed all around the seams. She looked at me, gave a wink, and started cutting. She had no pattern, simply a pair of scissors, needle, and thread. By the end of our visit, she had a beautiful tweed tam made for me. The material left over was tucked neatly away in a drawer for later use. Everything seemed to have more than one purpose, even the Eaton's catalogue. When Cliff and I were done reading it from cover to cover, it would end up in the outhouse and serve another purpose.

*Nancy*

There was limited access to 'stuff' in the 1940s. It was common to have two outfits, one for church and one for every day. Glass bottles needed to be saved and jam bottles were washed and reused. Today we have dollar stores, consignment stores, yard sales, online shopping, and even sites that gift gently used items. In my neighbourhood there are five-dollar stores within a five km radius. Today, we have unlimited access to anything we want.

Some people are still frugal, saving glass bottles to be reused when making pickles, using old cloth in quilts, and old towels for dog beds. People have hobbies where they collect items such as stamps, coins, or china. Saving items and collecting are normal today, as they were in the 1940s.

There is a relatively new mental health disorder called hoarding disorder today. Hoarding is not the same as being frugal or collecting. Collecting entails choosing items and organizing them in a certain way and does not negatively impact one's life. In comparison, the act of hoarding has no organization. Psychology Today (http:///www.psychgologytoday.com/ca/conditions/hoarding-disorder) explains that excessive amounts of items are acquired and stored in a very chaotic manner that can eventually lead to health and safety concerns. Items have little or no monetary value. Individuals who hoard feel compelled to acquire excessive quantities of items and feel a great sense of anxiety at the thought of discarding, recycling, or selling these items. Items may include things such as broken toys, plastic packaging, and even junk mail. Individuals with hoarding disorder have a strong attachment to their items and are comforted by acquiring and saving these items. In severe cases there is an inability to discard anything including items that have mildew, mold, and even rodent excrement.

Other characteristics of those who have hoarding disorder include:

1. Irrational beliefs about their 'things'.

Belief that all things need to be saved.

Belief that their things are treasure and have value.

Belief that they have a secret, and their things are valuable and no one else knows this.

2. Their living space eventually cannot be used for its intended purpose.

Items may be piled so high in a kitchen or bathroom that they cannot cook or use the facilities. This leads to unsafe and unhealthy living conditions.

3. Isolated and Lonely.

Distrust of relatives being in their space, touching their things, or talking about their mess/clutter. Suspicion that family may throw out their things/ treasure.

Individuals who hoard often refer to items as memories, and they associate an item with a memory that they cannot lose. A used paper napkin from their niece's birthday party, or a dirty clothespin their grandchild found in the garden are examples of items they associate as a memory. Some individuals who hoard have suffered a loss, typically the death of a loved one or loved ones, and they cannot bear the thought of parting with anything else, their items, and often their own garbage.

Hoarding can be cyclical with a pattern that is not easy to break. Individuals who hoard become caught in a behavioral loop which begins with acquiring excessive amounts of things; this acquisition brings them comfort and eases their anxiety in the short term. Family and friends notice their mess and offer help and encouragement to de clutter their home. The thought of parting with their items causes more stress and anxiety and to relieve this anxiety they acquire more items. The task of acquisition brings them comfort, is used to cope with feelings of anxiety, and the problem continues to get worse. Family and friends become frustrated, and the individual who is hoarding becomes suspicious of anyone who tries to help them address the issue. The behaviour may lead to strained relationships, isolation, and loneliness.

Hoarding disorder is more common in seniors, and when isolated and lonely with strained family relationships, they may become easy targets for financial abuse. A savvy manipulator can encourage their irrational beliefs and behaviours, convincing them that no one else understands them. They may manipulate the senior by assuring them that they will keep all their items and treasures safe long after their death. They may encourage outings that involve 'dumpster diving' or looking for 'treasures', in attempts to gain their trust, normalize their unhealthy behaviours for personal financial gain such as having them change their will making them sole beneficiary.

Hoarding disorder is difficult to treat and typically becomes worse over time. Hoarding poses severe safety and health issues the longer it continues, and what complicates the disorder is that Individuals who hoard do not see their beliefs and behaviours as a problem. Early intervention that is Cognitive Behavioural in nature has the greatest success rates. Cognitive Behavioural Therapy is a psychological treatment designed to change thoughts and behaviours. The goal of CBT is to foster understanding of emotions, thoughts, irrational beliefs, and unhealthy behavioral patterns, and encourage realistic thoughts and healthy behaviours.

Psychologist Michael Tompkins has written a book to

help family members deal with a loved one who suffers from hoarding disorder. *Digging Out* is a book that contains harm reduction strategies to help guide a loved one to healthier, safer ways to live.

Oh, by the way - if you are a collector of books, ask yourself why? Do you really plan on reading them again? Do you like how they look on a bookshelf as décor in your house? Or have you just never thought about passing them along for someone else to enjoy.

# Switchel

*Ruby*

Dad and the boys had left for the hay field as soon as the dew dried on the grass. The almanac had called for a wet summer that year, so there was a rush to get the hay in before the rain started. Being the only girl, I was stuck home with chores that I disliked, cooking, cleaning, using the wringer washer, and hanging the clothes out on the line. As I stood on my tip toes hanging shirts on the clothesline, I felt my cat Ginger rub up against my leg. I sat down on the grass beneath the clothesline and took a break from the heat, and all this ridiculous work. I felt a slight breeze blow and looked up at the clouds gently moving overhead. Ginger soon got bored and sauntered off towards the barn. I was finding lots of patterns in the clouds when Mum approached. She had a large molasses jug in her hand. 'Ruby, the men will need a cool drink in the hayfield, can you take this to them?' This was music to my ears! I would do anything to get out of these chores. I removed the cork of the molasses jug and peeked in, seeing not molasses but a liquid that was similar in colour. Mum said she would finish hanging the clothes out and off I went to the hayfield. They all greeted me with smiles of appreciation. Dad wasn't even grumpy with me, he exclaimed that the hayfield drink would give them energy to work until dark. My older brothers didn't look so happy about this, but when the day was done, I knew they'd take a quick dip in the brook to cool down. I took the empty stoneware jug back to Mum. She explained the great benefits of this 'hayfield punch'. She made the concoction with water, oats, molasses, some ginger, and cream of tartar. It didn't sound too appealing to me.

## Nancy

Haymaker's Punch is also called Hayfield Drink or Switchel. This vintage thirst quencher was around long before Gatorade and used to rehydrate and boost energy levels of field workers in the 19th and early 20th centuries. It was a common drink for those working in the fields and therefore was often referred to as Haymaker's Punch.

The origin of this drink is debatable. Some say the Amish brought it with them when they came to the US from Germany and Switzerland, while others say it originated in China. Most historians though believe switchel originated in the Caribbean and made its way north in the 18th century.

Switchel is a very simple non-alcoholic beverage and is known to have many health benefits. The cocktail eases inflammation, balances electrolytes, boosts the immune system and soothes digestion.

Recipes vary, and may include apple cider vinegar, lemon juice, and maple syrup. It can be enjoyed cold or at room temperature.

Switchel is making a comeback and is popular with today's hipsters (young people who view themselves as alternative to mainstream, are trend setters and up to date on the latest fashions). In 2015 companies began producing and distributing switchel, marketing it as nature's Gatorade and describing it as tasting pleasantly tart and not too sweet.

Oh, by the way, next time before you reach for the store-bought Gatorade which contains artificial colour and preservatives, why not make your own all-natural thirst quencher. There are lots of recipes online.

Robynne Elizabeth Miller is a Canadian Author who connects present with the past. She wrote the book *Pioneer Mixology* which includes the history on old fashion beverages including switchel. This book also includes quirky recipes that settlers and farmers drank in yesteryear. CHEERS!

*Photo Credit to Charlene Downey*

# The Dunce Hat

*Ruby*

We arrived at our one-room schoolhouse to discover our teacher, Miss Folkins, was not there. A male teacher was there in her place. I cannot recall his name, but I soon knew that he was nothing like our young, kind, caring and gentle Miss Folkins. He explained to us that Miss Folkins had pneumonia, and he would be our substitute teacher for the week. He obviously didn't arrive at the one room schoolhouse as early as Miss Folkins, as the fire was barely throwing any heat. Miss Folkins always made sure we arrived to a warm classroom, with a warm fire and a warm, caring person. This fellow seemed cold and stern, and he announced that he didn't put up with any tom foolery. I pulled my wool coat a bit tighter to protect myself from the cool air and his cold character. Reggie was the type of student that had trouble sitting still, so it wasn't long before Reggie was making his way closer to the stove.

'SIT DOWN!' came the command from the front of the room. Reggie, also a talker, began to explain, 'By gosh, I'm just going to put some wood in the fire.'

'SIT DOWN,' again echoed throughout the room.

Reggie sat back at his desk, and the room became quiet. I could sense I was not the only student feeling afraid. The quiet was broken with the sound of Reg drumming his fingers on his desk. A stern look came from the front of the room followed by, 'Young Man, you are in a classroom, not a barn yard. You will sit still and focus on academics. There is to be no talking, no walking around and no noise making.'

He then began teaching multiplication, although I'm not sure if he was teaching us or demanding we know the answers. He went around the room asking each of us questions. 'Ruby, what is 7 multiplied by 9?' I quickly answered '63'. He then moved on to Reggie. 'You there, what is 8 multiplied by 6?' Reggie began to mumble a bit and use his fingers to help with the answer. The teacher scoffed and said, 'You don't know the answer! You can't sit still, you make too much noise AND you are stupid, I have just the thing for you.' He rummaged through his bag with a smirk on his face and pulled out a pointy white hat with writing on it. He approached Reg and placed it on his head, instructing Reggie to keep it on for the remainder of the day.

'It's a dunce hat. You are a dunce, that means you are stupid, and when you are stupid you wear a hat like this.'

Miss Folkins would never talk to any of us like that. She helped us, spoke kindly to us, and made us feel we were contributing by asking the older students to help the younger students. She would ask Reggie to put wood in the fire so he could move around because she knew he had trouble sitting still. She said it was ok for any of us to count on our fingers or take as long as we needed to answer a question. She was a kind person and a good teacher. We were so happy when she returned.

*Nancy*

A dunce hat is a pointed white hat made with rolled up paper. It was used as a tool to discipline children who were disruptive or considered slow in the early 20th century. John Duns Scotus was the creator of the dunce hat and had the idea that the tall, pointy hat would inspire wisdom, however, it was typically used to ridicule, bully, embarrass and humiliate children in front of their peers. It was banned from schools in the 1950s.

Today's educators know, like Miss Folkins did, that children learn differently. Learning does not take place when a child is always required to sit still and be quiet. Learning does not happen when students fear their teacher.

Learning styles are methods of learning and the way a person takes in, understands, expresses, and remembers information. The three basic learning styles are Visual, Auditory, and Kinesthetic.

A visual learner will learn best by seeing. They understand maps, graphs, charts, and pictures. They may think in terms of pictures and learn best from visual displays including diagrams, illustrated textbooks, flipcharts, and handouts. They need to see the information they are learning.

Auditory learners like to hear the information, have verbal instructions, and listen. They learn best through verbal lectures, discussions, talking things through and listening to what others have said. Written information may have little meaning until it is heard. These learners benefit from reading text aloud and listening to others discuss the information.

Kinesthetic learners acquire information through experience and practice. They learn best by interacting with the environment around them and moving their body. They find it hard to sit still for long periods of time and become distracted by their need for activity and exploration.

When teachers are aware of learning styles, they can design lesson plans to make sure all their students have opportunity for success. They can teach to include all three learning styles. Teachers can improve their students' learning process, enhance student performance and outcomes by knowing about learning styles. A child who moves around a lot is likely a kinesthetic learner and therefore, it is important to provide opportunity to engage with the environment and provide hands on activities. When you look historically at the children who struggled in school, it was usually those hands-on learners who could not learn by sitting still. I'm glad we know more about the styles of learning so we can help all kids be a success and feel confident in their abilities.

Something else we know today is that individuals can be intelligent in a variety of ways. When we hear the term intelligence we may think of IQ, and whether our IQ is high or low. Whether we are smart does not depend on our IQ. In recent years other views on intelligence have emerged. Harvard Psychologist Howard Gardner has proposed the concept of Multiple Intelligence. The theory of multiple intelligence suggests that people are smart or intelligent in different ways. Gardner believes the traditional view on intelligence is rigid, restrictive, and limited. Gardner's theory suggests there are nine types of intelligence:

1. Visual-Spatial intelligence - those who are good at visualizing, can easily read maps, charts, and directions. They enjoy reading, can interpret graphs and charts well and can easily recognize patterns. You may find these people employed as architects and engineers.

2. Linguistic intelligence - those who are very good with words when writing and speaking. These individuals are great readers and writers. They explain things well and use humour when telling stories. They are great with words. You may find these people employed as lawyers or playwrights.

3. Logical intelligence - those who are good at math, reasoning, analysing, and problem solving. They enjoy abstract ideas, doing experiments and using numbers and logic. They are drawn to professions such as accounting, banking, and research.

4. Kinesthetic Intelligence - those who have excellent hand eye coordination and are skilled at moving their body and performing actions. Dancers and athletes would fall into this category. They enjoy creating with their hands and remember by doing rather than listening and seeing. They are drawn to professions such as firefighting, surgical operating, building, and constructing. They are productive and content when they can use their hands and move around their environment.

5. Musical intelligence - those who are good at rhythms and sounds, have a strong appreciation for music, are skilled at music composition and /or performance. They enjoy singing, musical instruments, and remembering songs and melodies. They have a rich understanding of music structure. These are the music teachers, singers, and performers.

6. Interpersonal intelligence - those who can understand and interact with people. They are good at assessing emotions, motivations, and the intentions of those around them. They relate well to people, communicate well, recognize nonverbal communication (body language) and see situations from different perspectives. These people can be found in roles such as

therapists, nurses, and sales. They easily build relationships.

7. Intrapersonal intelligence - those who are very aware of their own feelings, emotions, and motivations. They are self-reflective and sometimes day dreamers. They excel at knowing their own personal strengths and have excellent self-awareness. These people may be drawn to such occupations as inventors or artists, and they often prefer self-employment. They know what they want because they know themselves.

8. Naturalistic intelligence - those who are in tune with nature and interested in the environment, botany, biology, and animals. They enjoy outside activities such as camping, hiking, and exploring nature. They are drawn to hobbies and employment that involve nature. Fishermen, gardeners, and biologists are only a few occupations that match those who have a naturalistic intelligence.

9. Existential intelligence - those who can delve deep into questions about life and existence. They question the meaning of life and constantly consider how their actions may influence the future. They are global thinkers who have interest and concern for others. Those with existential intelligence are usually found in careers such as theology and philosophy.

Knowledge of Gardner's multiple intelligence theory assists educators in building lessons that empower all students to learn. A variety of learning activities and assessment strategies builds interest and confidence while supporting every student.

Some teachers have been teaching like this for years, with a natural ability to get to know each of their students and build on their natural strength and talent. I suspect Miss Folkins had a high level of interpersonal intelligence and could quickly sense what motivated each of her students. She knew some needed to move around, use their fingers for counting, and thrived when they felt they could contribute by being responsible for tasks within the classroom.

Canadian author and teacher Joyce VC Forbes has written a book called *Perseverance, Pranks and Pride - Tales of a one room schoolhouse*. Her book includes how students and teachers coped with issues such as not having electricity, an outhouse, pranks, and the pride of a schoolhouse being the heart of the community. The one-room schoolhouse provided an education that produced independent, resourceful, and caring citizens.

Oh, by the way, both my mom and dad went to the same one room schoolhouse in Titusville. The picture below shows my father, Harold in the middle with other classmates in the early 1950s. This photograph was taken by his teacher, Miss Folkins.

*Photo credit to Florence (Folkins) Elliott*

# Revenge

*Ruby*

My house was directly beside the Titus Hill cemetery in Titusville, New Brunswick. The land for this cemetery was donated by the Titus family in the early 1800s. John Titus owned over 1,000 acres in the area, and approximately two acres was donated to be a non-denominational cemetery where Baptists, Methodists and Catholics would all be buried together. The cemetery was over 100 years old when I was young and although it was filled with gravestones and grave markers, it was also my playground. I would walk through the stones, appreciating the beauty of the rose bushes that grew at the top of the hill, and the ground flox that resembled a pink blanket throughout the cemetery in early summer. In May, there would be bluets, and Cliff and I used to pick bouquets of these delicate flowers for Mum on Mother's Day. I'm sure my love of books, reading and genealogy came from so much time playing in the cemetery. My cat Ginger would often accompany me, rubbing up against the stones as I read the names and dates. The stones were all so different - some had lambs on them, some were white, some grey, and some were even toppled over, making it difficult to read the names on these gravestones.

What intrigued me the most was the biggest stone at the very top of the hill, a tombstone bigger than the rest with the name Richard Burns, who died in 1848. Mum told the story that Richard Burns left Titusville in the early 1800s after a row with John Titus. John thought a lot of himself, he owned lots of land, and Titusville was named after his family. The story goes that Mr. Titus talked down to Mr. Burns and was disrespectful with insinuations that he was not destined for anything but being a farmer on a small piece of land, shovelling manure. What Titus didn't know is that Richard Burns had a dream. One day Mr. Burns had enough of John Titus' bullying and announced he was leaving Titusville and moving on to 'greener pastures'. Richard promised he would be back to make sure his tombstone was the biggest one in Titus Hill cemetery. Mr. Burns was scoffed at and considered no threat to the big shot John Titus. John was confident that the biggest stone/stones would be for the Titus family, not the poor Burns family. Richard left and was not heard of again.

Richard Burns moved to the States and opened and operated a very successful furniture shop in Boston, Massachusetts. He had a family who worked alongside him in his store for more than 30 years. They were obviously informed of Richard's wishes, and when he died in 1948, his family returned to Titusville to bury Richard and to erect the largest stone, at the very top of the hill, in the Titus Hill cemetery that bore the name RICHARD BURNS!

The more common story is that Richard Burns never forgot where he came from and upon his death wanted to go home, be buried where he was born, where his family originated from. It's just a coincidence that his stone was the biggest and placed at the very top of the hill of the cemetery. A story of a man who left, became successful, rich, and wanted to be laid to rest in a place that he loved, and provided the foundation for his success.

## Nancy

Which story is true? I'm not sure, maybe both. I do know that Richard Burns' tombstone has been talked about since his death in 1948.

It is human nature when we are wronged to want to get revenge. Revenge is the rumination of desire to inflict pain on someone for an injury or injustice suffered at their hands, inflicting injury back for their wrongdoing. Revenge is usually associated with aggression and violence.

Thoughts of revenge are a natural human instinct, and happens when trust has been damaged, or someone has hurt an individual or their family. It is often believed that a vengeful act or actions will be the emotional release that bring closure and restore joy and happiness, however, the benefit received after a vengeful act is usually short lived and causes feelings of shame and guilt and brings darkness. Jennifer Breheny Wallace wrote an article in 2017 for the Washington Post (washingtonpost.com/national/health-science) titled 'Why Getting Even May Make You Feel Worse in the Long Run'. She reports that research suggests people who take revenge by executing pain or harm in the form of violence usually feel worse. An eye for an eye leaves two people blind, with the original victim becoming the perpetrator, a characteristic they likely never identified with.

The desire for revenge is not necessarily detrimental, but the way one copes with this desire can be. Thoughts of vengeance can rob a person of a happy life and take away the ability to be mindful and enjoy the present.

The best way to manage feelings of revenge is to redirect

the focus on success. Be kind, be caring, and strive for growth. Being authentic and genuine will show true character, foster friendships, and a sense of meaning. Getting on with life, moving forward and having a better life than the person that wronged you is the best revenge.

Here are some tangible things to do when you have been wronged and have a desire for revenge:

1. Know these feelings are normal. Injustice causes the body to feel uncomfortable, anxious, and angry. Acceptance of these raw emotions can be helpful.

2. Create a dialogue of facts and don't shy away from talking. When an injustice occurs, the victim can feel like they have done something wrong, causing confusion and shame. The aggressor counts on this narrative as they want to be seen as the good guy and the victim as the bad guy and will often spread rumours to have others see the victim in a negative light. It's imperative to speak up and correct misinformation.

3. Put strong boundaries in place and limit contact with the toxic person. Bullies get power from their abusive attitude and behaviour, so removing oneself from their life, removes their power. Know you cannot control their behaviour, but you can protect yourself by having a firm boundary in place with little or no contact when possible.

4. Talk about your successes, especially if you need to be around the toxic person. Chances are they have targeted you because they are jealous. Their abusive behaviour is an attempt to stunt your growth, hurt your feelings, and take away your confidence. Instead of being motivated to improve their own life, bullies will

attempt to bring others down to feel powerful. Simply being aware of this is helpful. Being happy, content, and confident will exasperate the intimidator.

5. Spend time with those who love and support you, are fun and enjoy your company. It's disappointing and heart breaking but sometimes family members are the bullies and the toxic people in your life. Find friends to take their place and know other people also have bullies in their family too. I've heard lately of celebrations that include friends and not family. 'Friendsgiving' is a term I recently heard that means a thanksgiving dinner with friends and not family. Family needs to know that if their behaviour is toxic, there will be consequences and the need for firm boundaries. You need to know its ok to walk away from people who are damaging, even when those people are family.

6. Seek positive outcomes to counteract the desire for revenge. Celebrate every success you have, knowing that becoming a better person and having a better life will irritate your offender.

Taking revenge and focusing on negative, hurtful acts of violence brings negativity into one's life. It's best to let Karma handle it. The person will get what they deserve, and you don't need to do a thing.

The better form of revenge is not violent or aggressive in nature. A better revenge will transform a grudge into a successful power play. Using the desire for retaliation as a motivator to prove the doubters wrong, and becoming more successful will hurt the offender more, and the legacy lasts longer. Just go to the top of Titus Hill Cemetery and see whose name is on the biggest stone at the very top of the hill 175 years later!

Dr. AJ Rolls normalizes the desire for revenge and provides an alternative to the typical negative revenge we are all familiar with in his book 'Positive Revenge'. He explains how to channel the desire for revenge into healthy ways that benefits the victim and the bully.

Oh, by the way, if you want to visit Titus Hill Cemetery, it is in Titusville, New Brunswick, approximately 30 minutes from Saint John. Be sure to go to the top to see the largest gravestone.

# Fishing

*Ruby*

My brother Ken was helping me dig for worms behind the cow barn. It had just rained, so the soil was loose, the worms were plentiful, and there was lots of water in the nearby brook. It was a great morning for fishing.

Dad walked by carrying a pitchfork heading for the manure pile. He asked what we were up to.

'Goin' fishin',' I exclaimed.

Dad laughed and said, 'You'll be lucky to catch an old shoe!'

Once we had lots of worms in our small can, Ken showed me how to select the best branch from a tree that would act as my fishing pole. He said to select a branch from a young tree that was springy and flexible and about the diameter of my thumb and four to five feet long. The first branch I chose was too big according to Ken. I was getting scratched to pieces trying to find the right size branch. It wasn't long though before I found the perfect branch. Ken had his shiny red jack knife in his pocket and used it to remove the branch from the tree, then removed all the side branches and leaves, and my fishing pole was ready. I tied a piece of string to it and put a hook with one of the worms we had dug on the end. I was proud of myself for creating my new home-made fishing pole and was sure I was going to catch loads of fish, enough to feed everyone supper, and even have some leftover for my cat Ginger.

Ken and I sat on the bank of the brook all morning, enjoying the warm air and the light breeze that blew the tall grass along the meadow. We didn't talk a whole lot, simply enjoying each other's company as we waited for the fish to bite. We could hear the cows off in the distance giving a gentle moo every now and again, and the tinkle of the cowbell in the breeze. The air smelled of summer, a mix of wildflowers, trees, the moist earth underfoot and the rose bushes that grew wild along the brook.

By mid-afternoon we packed it in and headed back to the house. Dad was right, we didn't catch a thing, not even an old shoe, but somehow it still felt like a great way to spend the day.

## Nancy

Today fishing is still a hobby enjoyed by many. Expensive fishing rods have replaced the tree branch fishing pole, and translucent fishing line has replaced the string. Today it is easier to buy fishing equipment and it's a big business for outfitters and fishing guides.

Fishing is an activity that helps foster good mental health by allowing individuals to meet some of the basic needs discussed earlier like fun, freedom, connection, and accomplishment. It is also a mindful activity.

Mindful is a present-day word for being in the moment, being present and noticing what is going on around you. Often anxiety happens when we spend too much time thinking about the past or the future and not enough time being in the present moment. Our brain becomes overwhelmed if we spend long periods of time ruminating on or overthinking about experiences from the past. Things we should have said or done, mistakes we made, injustices we experienced and being wronged by others are just a few things we humans tend to obsess and worry about. Overthinking can cause anxiety, and then anxiety causes more overthinking. A cycle that's difficult to break.

Spending too much time thinking about the future is also overwhelming to the brain. It's normal to have goals for the future, and an action plan to accomplish these goals. It's normal to schedule events for the future, however, if we spend too much time wondering about future outcomes that we cannot control, we can easily become overwhelmed and paralysed by anxiety. If we spend too much time scheduling things far in advance or rehearsing for the future, our mental health will suffer. The fear/worry centre, also called the amygdala, lives in the temporal lobe of the brain, close to the base of the skull behind the ears. This part of the brain becomes activated, and thoughts of the future become worries which can lead to catastrophizing and extreme negative thinking and worry. Worrying robs us of today and prevents us from experiencing beauty, peace, and joy that the present moment has to offer. Chronic catastrophizing and worrying can impact physical health too and may lead to ulcers, heart issues and auto immune disorders.

The ability to think about the past long enough to reflect on how you can do better or behave differently is an important skill to have. Afterall, we learn from our mistakes. The ability to think about the future long enough to plan and be organized is needed to build a successful life.

If we spend most of our time in the present moment, we essentially teach our brain to be calm. There is no danger or need to worry usually in the present moment. If we spend time in the past or future, we will be more anxious, but if we spend more time in the present moment, we will be calmer. Spending time in the present moment means we notice what's going on around us at the current moment. What do we see? What do we hear? What do we smell? What do we notice within ourselves? How is my breathing? These simple mindful questions draw our attention to the present and can help us be calm and remain calm. A simple yet important concept to prevent anxiety and manage anxiety is to be in the present moment, and just notice. Think about Ruby being quiet as she sat and waited for a fish to bite. If she was anxious over the past or worried about the future, she would not have been able to sit still and simply enjoy her day as she did, despite not catching any fish.

A therapeutic intervention that can be done anywhere is 'noticing'. Take a breath and notice how you are feeling. What's your breathing like? Notice that. Now look around slowly. What do you see? Name five things you see as you look around slowly without analysis or judgement. If you see a tree you say, 'I see a tree' not, 'I see a tree. I wonder how old that tree is. How many animals live in it? I wonder if it will fall down during the next windstorm?'. The activity is to notice the tree and move on to the next thing. After noticing five things you can see, just listen. What can you hear? Can you hear four different sounds if you really listen, again without judgement or analysis. Think 'I hear a bird singing' and not 'I hear a bird singing. What kind of bird is that? I wonder how early that bird starts making that noise and how many hours a day it sings for?' Train your mind to think 'I hear a bird' and move on to what else you may hear. Then notice three things you can smell. This one is easier when you are in nature. Notice your breathing then notice again what's going on around you. Go slow and just notice. This is training the brain to be calm and present.

Nick Trenton authors the book *Stop Overthinking*, which details more techniques on how to quiet the mind and be present. He has a MA in Behavioural Psychology, and his book is filled with loads of practical strategies on stress free living.

Oh, by the way, my uncle Ken continued his love of fishing well into his eighties. He had a cottage on the Miramichi River in New Brunswick where he could fish almost right from his doorstep.

*Photo credit to Betty Ann Ryan*

*Photo credit to Charlene Downey*

# The Winter Blues

*Ruby*

In was mid-November and the days were short and the nights long. I was going to school in the dark and coming home in the dark. It was cold and damp, but Mum knew how to make things brighter for us all. She would have the fire on, so we felt warm as soon as we got home from school. Mum would cook and bake all day and the kitchen always had a comforting aroma. The smell of cinnamon in winter, pickling spices in the fall and of course simple white bread and pan rolls that was always a treat to the olfactory senses. Each night when we had supper, she would set the table like it was an occasion, with pickles, cheese, the glass molasses jar, homemade biscuits. Everything looked perfect. This night Mum had made beans with molasses, fried ham, and potato scallop, and it smelled heavenly.

The wind was howling down the stovepipe as Mum fixed my plate like she always did. As she put it in front of me, Dad scoffed and told Mum she shouldn't dote on me so much.

'Now Art, she's not going to be little much longer, let me make a fuss over her,' said Mum. Dad just shook his head. He seemed cranky as he looked out the window and expressed his frustration of how cold it was already, with the Farmer's Almanac calling for lots of snow and storms this year. I was eager to get started on my supper and announced that my meal needed some butter. Dad reached over with a knife full of hard butter and dropped it on my plate. It was hard from being in the icebox and I couldn't even break it up. It just sat there on top of my food, and I started to cry. 'Why are you crying now?' Dad raised his voice at me, which only made me cry harder. Of course, Mum came to my rescue, and assured me she would be able to cut the butter up. Mum's gentle voice always made things better. My meal was perfect again, with butter spread evenly on my scallop. 'Ruby don't let your dad upset you, he is cranky because it's so dark out, and there is still lots of work to be done on the farm - work doesn't stop just because the sun goes down.' Mom continued, 'Art, one day our five children will be grown, and we will miss these times. One day we won't have anything to do but enjoy our retirement, maybe have a small house that's not too much work.' Dad cheered up a bit at the thought of less work and brighter days to come.

## Nancy

In New Brunswick in the 1940s and still today, November days are bleak. The leaves and flowers have died and the general colour outside is gray. It's dark until 8 am and the sun goes down well before 5 pm. Beautiful flowers and long bright days will not return for many months, and the days are short and the nights long and cold. It is common for people to get the winter blues during these dark winter months and some people can develop a condition called Seasonal Affective Disorder (SAD). This is different than feeling blue. SAD interrupts daily life and functioning. SAD is a type of depression triggered by the change of seasons. Symptoms of SAD begin in the fall (typical onset is in November) and last until spring. Symptoms include feelings of hopelessness, very low energy, being tired, sluggish, oversleeping, feelings of sadness, sugar cravings, low mood, and disinterest in activities that usually bring joy.

It is believed that this seasonal depression is caused by the reduction of sunlight. Reduced levels of sunlight can disrupt the body's internal rhythm along with brain chemicals such as serotonin. Serotonin is a substance in the body that fosters happiness and satisfaction and influences learning, memory, sleep, hunger, and mood. Lack of serotonin is believed to play a role in depression and sleep issues which impact mood and lead to feelings of depression. The balance of melatonin in the body is disrupted which in turn disrupts sleep patterns and mood. Those with Seasonal Affective Disorder tend to have negative thought patterns about winter. It's not clear, though, if these negative thoughts contribute to SAD or if SAD contributes to the negative thoughts.

The risk of a SAD diagnosis increases if there is a family history of depression or if an individual has other mental health issues such as anxiety or depression. Those who live far from the equator have less access to sunlight and vitamin D especially in the winter, so geographic location is a risk factor itself. Risk of SAD also increases with age and is more common in females. There are behaviours that can prevent Seasonal Depression and help manage it as well. Getting outside every day, eating healthy food, exercising, social engagement and participating in psychotherapy can all be helpful. Basic things that may be overlooked such as drinking plenty of water and respecting sleep and work/life balance is also important. Seasonal Affective Disorder can be diagnosed by your medical doctor, and once diagnosed, they may recommend certain types of medicine to assist.

If you are diagnosed with SAD, or even if you are just feeling the winter blues, there are behaviours that tend to make it worse:

1. Isolating yourself in your home, disengaging from friends and connections will increase feelings of loneliness and increase symptoms of depression.
2. Keeping the curtains closed and blinds drawn will also bring on feelings of isolation and loneliness and keeps out any sunlight that may be helpful and uplifting.
3. Alcohol makes depression worse.

If you struggle with the winter blues or seasonal depression, there are interventions you can employ to help. Here are a few:

1. Your healthcare provider is a good place to start. Your medical doctor may be able to suggest the best course of action depending on your individual circumstances. Your family physician can evaluate if medication may be beneficial, and which type of medication is best. Vitamin D may also be prescribed, which is an over-the-counter supplement. The consensus is most people north of Boston, Massachusetts, are deficient in Vitamin D, especially in winter months.
2. Light therapy has been found to reduce symptoms of Seasonal Depression. Light therapy involves sitting close to a special light box that mimics sunlight for about 30 minutes a day. It is theorized that this type of light, which is brighter than indoor light, but not as bright as direct sunlight causes a chemical change in the brain which lifts mood and reduces symptoms

of seasonal depression.

3. Psychotherapy helps individuals understand and recognize their thoughts, feelings, and emotions. A Licensed Counselling Therapist (LCT) can help with developing strategies and a plan to prevent SAD or cope with symptoms of seasonal depression. An LCT will help you set realistic goals for yourself and encourage small tasks each day to strengthen your mental health.

4. Be realistically positive. Negative thoughts and negative statements can bring negative feelings. Try to remain positive and realistic. Reframe negative thoughts to ones that are more realistic and positive. For example, 'I hate winter. It's always dark and dreary and I'm going to be miserable until summer,' can be reframed to something that is more realistically positive such as, 'I prefer warmer weather and look forward to summer, but there are bright sunny days in winter that are nice and I can enjoy the beauty of winter on these days'. The brain chemicals that are responsible for uplifting mood are stimulated when positive words are used.

How we speak in these cases is important, too. There is new lingo that young people use that is not recognized as a positive response in the brain. Instead of responding to thank you with 'you're welcome' or 'my pleasure' in recent years you may have heard the response, 'no worries.' The brain interprets this as two negatives. No and Worry. The same is the case for double negatives that translate to a positive idea like, I won't hate winter. Here the brain hears WON'T. and HATE. Reframing your thoughts and words can be a tremendous strategy to help uplift mood.

Unrealistic positivity is not helpful. Today some call this

extreme positive focus toxic positivity. Extreme positivity is not realistic or sustainable and can be just as damaging as catastrophic or negative thinking. An example of toxic positive thinking might be, 'I am going to wake up every day with joy to embrace the winter months' or 'I am going to be super happy, and every day will be wonderful'. This is not a realistic statement and, on the days, when you wake up tired or sick the brain sees this as a failure to meet the expectation that you set. Stick with realistic positive thoughts.

The brain is impacted by thoughts and words. There is a section of the brain that is hard-wired to keep us safe by always scanning our environment for threats. In caveman days this part of the brain was always on guard looking for the threat of a saber tooth tiger. Today this part of the brain still exists despite the extinction of saber tooth tigers and our evolution from caveman to modern man. It is still the centre where worry lives and can become activated by hearing hostile or negative words. Even one negative word can activate this fear centre. Negative words cause the brain to release a stress hormone into the bloodstream and when there is no real threat it negatively impacts our mental health. When this fear or worry centre is activated the other parts of our brain can shut down which impairs our executive functioning, making it difficult to use logic and reasoning. The opposite happens when we think or hear positive words. Our executive functioning is activated and strengthened while our fear center remains inactive.

If you're interested to know more on this topic, Norman Rosenthal, MD, is a psychiatrist who wrote a book called *Winter Blues: Everything You Need to Know to Beat Seasonal*

*Affective Disorder.*

Oh, by the way - if you can't get outside in the cold winter months, at least open the curtains and the blinds, and let the sunshine in!

*Photo credit to Betty Ann Ryan*

*Photo credit to Elizabeth Crouchman*

# Boundaries and Narcissists

*Ruby*

I was up early, and Mum made sure I was as clean as a whistle with a bow in my hair. I was going to town with my Aunt Ethel and her husband Morris. Morris had a big fancy car, and I couldn't wait to check out the City Market. I enjoyed the architecture, decorated windows, and meeting all the shop owners selling their wares. Mum gave me some money she had squirreled away from selling eggs, and I was excited at what I might buy. The possibilities and excitement made the trip to town go very fast.

We parked at the top of King Street and meandered down the steep street overlooking the harbour, stopping in all the shops, meeting people, and exchanging pleasantries with the store owners. Morris knew lots of people in town, and everyone we met stopped to talk with us. I decided I was looking for a big colorful lollipop to spend my money on. As we neared the market there was a small store that looked more like a shed with a sign that said, 'My treasures'. I could see some shiny things in the window and wondered if they sold suckers. Morris said we shouldn't go in there as the owner was a bit 'off', and it was best to stay clear of him. I had no idea what this meant, but Aunt Ethel must have seen the look on my face and announced that we all would be going in to look around. Morris spoke up and said, 'Ok just for a minute, in search of a sucker, and then we are moving along.'

We entered the shop, and it was dark and smelled funny. The shop owner didn't look up as he smoked a cigarette behind the counter where he stood. The place was filled with tiny trinkets, and old rusty things with no organization at all. I was afraid I would knock something over; it was so full of stuff. I carefully walked around the shop, making sure not to bump anything. I saw three colourful suckers wrapped in plastic up by the counter next to the shop owner and decided that was exactly what I would buy.

'I will take one sucker please,' I said to the man. The shop owner looked me up and down with a look of suspicion in his eyes.

'That'll be five cents.' I dug through my change purse and gave him a dime, took my sucker, and waited for my change. The man looked Ethel up and down much like he had looked at me and said, 'And what are you buying?'

'Nothing today sir,' Ethel said with a smile, 'but we enjoyed looking through your shop'. The man was now glaring at all of us, and I was just waiting for my change.

'I saw you steal from me. Don't think I didn't see you slip one of my expensive items in your purse. I want you to get out of my store and don't come back.'

Aunt Ethel tried to reason with the man. 'Oh no sir, you must be mistaken, we didn't take a thing, you do have some lovely items here in your store though.'

'You people think I'm stupid, you come in here and steal. I know your type. You are a bunch of thieves and I want you out of my store.'

Morris had enough. 'We will leave, and never come back

as soon as you give my niece the change you owe her.'

'Oh, you're trying to steal more from me now are you… the kid gave me a nickel and you owe me for the trinkets the lady put in her purse, so you actually owe me!'

At that Morris ushered us out of the store, as the man lit up another cigarette with a smirk on his face. I was very confused and felt scared. Why was this man so mean? Why did he not give me my change? All we wanted to do was buy a sucker, and why did he accuse us of being thieves? I felt ashamed even though I knew I did nothing wrong. Morris's face was flushed, and I could tell he was mad. He stooped down and said 'Ruby, that man is a criminal with no integrity, and the best way to handle a situation like that, the only way really, is to stay away from him. He has something very wrong with him and is not a nice person. I will give you the five cents he owes you. I've had dealings with that man before. Carl Phillips is a very unhappy man and instead of trying to be happy, he focuses on making other people miserable. He finds it funny when he steals, then accuses the innocent of being the thief. We won't let him ruin our day. He is stuck in his tiny little shed, selling junk as treasure, and feeling miserable.'

We then skipped across the street, heading towards the Market. I perked up quick as we entered the City Market and saw all the bustling and decorations. People chatted with us and were friendly and excited to see us. Everyone wanted to meet me and talked to me with gentle voices and enthusiastic eyes. I didn't let that nasty man ruin my day at all!

*Nancy*

'It takes all kinds of people to make the world go around' as the saying goes. There are kind people, happy people, sad people, and difficult people. Today we know about personality disorders, and one of the most damaging personality disorders is *narcissistic personality disorder.* NPD is a mental health condition in which a person believes they are better and deserve more than everyone else. They have an unreasonably high sense of importance and lack the ability to have compassion for others. They are typically very unhappy people that will do whatever they can to disrupt others' happiness. More recently we know there are even different types of narcissists:

1. *Overt Narcissists* are easier to spot. They are loud bullies that believe they are right even when they are wrong. They blatantly exploit others, and they accuse people of doing evil or bad things that they themselves have done. They have an entitled sense that the world owes them, and believe they deserve special treatment. They are takers and thrive on controlling and abusing others. They feed their power by putting others down, being abusive and nasty just like Carl Phillips.

2. *Covert Narcissists* do not always act with aggression. Although they do expect special treatment and feel entitled to have what others have, they often see themselves as a martyr or even a victim. These narcissists are usually, but not always, female. When their controlling, demanding behaviour does not get them what they want they use tears, playing the victim to get what they want while manipulating those around them. They

generally do not have compassion for others and their behaviour and motives are self-serving. They will have some people who they are close with, however these people need to act in a way that serves the narcissist and feeds their sense of entitlement.

3. *Sociopathic Narcissists* have no respect for laws and will lie to police, lawyers, and judges. They believe they are above the law and do not need to follow any rules of society. They believe they can take whatever they want without consequences. They have no remorse, and the more they hurt others the more powerful they feel.

Narcissists have no accountability or remorse. They spare no one from their abusive self-serving nature, including their own parents, children, co-workers, and friends. They profit at the expense of others and take advantage of the vulnerable. They think nothing of taking money from elderly, sick parents or manipulating parents to change their wills making them sole beneficiary. They see these despicable actions as a powerful win. If they are ever held accountable for their abusive and exploitive nature, they make it their mission to bring down the person that speaks up.

It is extremely challenging to have a relationship with a narcissist due to their need for control and their dismissive nature towards others. They have no interest in celebrating the accomplishments of others and are terrible listeners because they have no interest in what others have to say. They display toxic behaviours and have many tactics to never be accountable while shifting blame and responsibility to others.

Although narcissists believe they deserve and are entitled to special treatment, deep down they are very insecure and have low self-worth. They are very sensitive to any criticism and any perceived criticism will lead to an angry outburst. They are jealous of others and cannot connect with many people in a meaningful way.

How do we get along with people who have this mental health disorder? The best way to deal with a narcissist is to STAY AWAY, keep your distance, and do not engage with them. If you have a family member that is a narcissist it can be very difficult to manage. When possible do not engage or engage as little as possible.

Narcissists hate the word 'No'. They typically won't ask you a yes or no question, instead issuing demands and providing you with instructions to follow. The best approach is a strong boundary, keeping your distance when possible and saying 'no', without any explanation. Explanations are not met as negotiation, but perceived as a way to manipulate, so no explanation is best when dealing with a narcissist, simply use the word no, or no thank you. Do not feel the need to be extra nice to keep them from freaking out. It is not your responsibility to help them change. They will not change, and sadly, have no interest in being a better person.

One of the most important things when you are in the presence of a narcissist is knowing how to keep yourself safe. Your patience and kindness will not help them. They view kindness as weakness and the vulnerable as easy prey. What you need to do is have strong boundaries and get out of the relationship when possible.

The good news as reported by Stephanie Eckelkamp

and Madeleine Haase in their article from September 2022 (prevention.com/health/mental-health/g19876574/narcissistic-personality-disorder) is that less than 5% of the population have narcissistic personality disorder (NPD) which means 95% of people have good intentions and care about others. Knowing how to recognize individuals with this destructive personality disorder can help you protect yourself from their wrath of manipulation, abuse, and exploitation. Narcissists may seem knowledgeable and even charming at first. They may love bomb and say lovely things to draw in their victims. Their abuse may stary slowly, but one sign will be gaslighting: they will blame their own behaviour on those who notice it, just like Carl Phillips, blaming his customers of stealing when he in fact was not providing the change owed to my mom. Narcissists will be drawn to kind empathic people, who sometimes are so selfless they do not recognize the one-sided toxic relationship until they are too damaged to leave the relationship, believing that all the issues are the victim's fault. By setting healthy boundaries you can keep yourself safe from these toxic individuals.

Linda Martineq-Lewi is a psychologist and licensed therapist who understands how draining a narcissist can be and how liberating it is to walk away. Linda's book *Freeing Yourself from the Narcissist in Your Life* discusses how to spot narcissistic traits and how to protect yourself from the destructive, self-serving behaviours of the narcissist.

Oh, by the way Carl Phillips is a fictitious name given to the shop owner my mom, Ethel and Morris encountered that day.

*Photo credit to Kelley Joyce-Floyd*

# Grief and Loss

*Ruby*

It was late in the fall when I left for school, there were flurries in the air. I was worried as my cat Ginger hadn't been home in days. I knew tom cats roam and could be gone awhile, but I had a strange feeling something was wrong. It was getting cold out, and Ginger loved laying in the hay close to the cows in the barn on cold days. Ginger loved it when Dad would milk the cows and squirt milk directly into his mouth. He would lap it up like it was the best treat in the world. Ginger was a barn cat, but I would sneak him into the house whenever I could. He loved my feather tick bed and snuggling up with me as I wrote in my diary each night.

I thought about Ginger all day at school, and raced home when school was done, hoping to find Ginger waiting for me. When I arrived home, I found Mum in the kitchen by the stove. There was something she was tending too on the floor wrapped in a towel. My heart sank. Mum explained that Ginger had made his way home, but he was in rough shape. He had been in a cat fight and one of his ears was badly torn, he could barely walk, and he had a terrible gash in his neck. I laid on the floor for hours and was thankful Mum let Ginger stay by the fire. Dad was late getting home that night and when he came through the door, I ran to him and told him what had happened to Ginger. Dad loved cats as much as I did and when he said, 'Ruby, Ginger will be ok,' his eyes said something different. Ginger died later that evening and I cried until I fell asleep. Mum said I didn't have to go to school the next day, and my older brother helped me bury Ginger behind the barn. I was devastated.

*Nancy*

Grief is a normal emotion when a loss is experienced, whether the death of someone we love or a beloved pet. Grief can feel like pain even though there is no physical injury. It can feel like a broken heart. It can feel like we cannot go on. When the sun comes up the next morning, we can feel shocked that life is carrying on. How can the sun come up after this terrible thing has happened? How dare the sun come up! How dare life go on! Why did God let this happen? No one understands what this feels like! I am alone! I will never be the same! I am permanently damaged!

We once thought that grief had 5 stages, with denial being first, then anger, followed by bargaining, depression, and acceptance, and it could take up to a year to complete all the stages, with an assumption that we should be healed at that time. We now know that grief is not linear and does not have a timeline to completion. There is no right way to grieve and there is no timeline for grief. The sorrow and suffering grief brings will be different for everyone. Some people explain grief like it's a black hole in their heart that will never be filled and all they can do is slowly build a life around the black hole.

There are things you can do when you are grieving that can be helpful:

1. Allow yourself time to be sad and to cry. Cry a lot if you need to.

2. Don't pressure yourself to feel any differently than how you feel.

3. Have small goals each day. Eat something, drink water, get a little fresh air, and get some sleep.

4. Engage in things that promote self-care. This will be different for everyone and could include a bubble bath, a coffee with a friend, ice cream, or listening to some favourite music to name a few.

If you know someone who is grieving, there are things you can do to be helpful:

1. Know that you cannot take their grief away. You can be with them and support them as they are grieving, but you cannot take their pain away.

2. Take them food, flowers, or a card to offer your condolences and support.

3. When you talk to someone who is grieving expect them to be sad. You don't need to say anything, just listen if they want to talk.

4 Invite them to do things. They may say 'no'. and that's ok. Keep asking. They will appreciate that you are thinking of them.

*The Heart Does Break* is a book featuring several Canadian authors writing about their own grief. A heartbreaking, comforting collection of true stories about grief and mourning.

*Photo credit to Jacqueline Carr*

*Photo credit to Jacqueline Carr*

*Photo credit to Jacqueline Carr*

# Anger

*Ruby*

I don't know how my mum did it, but our house was always spotless, always had a warm fire burning, the wood box was full, there was always cookies or biscuits in the oven, and our clothes were always clean, which was a chore having 4 boys and me in the house. She washed all the clothes on Monday in the wringer washer and hung them out to dry on the clothesline even on the coldest of days. She always had time for visitors and looked forward to serving guests tea and a plate of sweets. Mum took pride in her house and her family. When we left the house for church or community gatherings, we were all shiny and in our Sunday best. Being the only girl, Mum dressed me in ruffes, frills and lace, and the final touch was always a bow in my hair. As I grew older, I knew I was not like other girls who liked lace and pretty things. I had no interest in cooking or cleaning and I did not like having a bow in my hair. I knew how hard Mum worked and how she delighted in dressing me up and showing me off. I was her only girl, so I usually didn't complain. I preferred history, books, and wearing comfortable clothes. I couldn't see the point in wasting time cleaning or cooking for hours when there were books to read, and knowledge to be gained.

On this Sunday morning, we were preparing for church and a box social that would be held after the service. All the woman and girls in the community packed a box lunch for two.

The girls at school had been talking about it all week. They'd pack a delicious lunch, maybe a sandwich, a date square, or a piece of apple pie. The final touch was decorating the lunch box with ribbon and a colourful bow. The boxes were auctioned off and the highest bidder would have lunch with the girl who prepared the lunch. One of the boys at school was completely smitten with my friend Ruth and had been asking what color ribbon she would be putting on her box. I had written in my diary the night before how foolish I thought the whole thing was and couldn't wait for it to be over. I was not participating, however I did know that others thought it was fun, so I would remain quiet about my feelings on the subject. I'd have lunch with Mum, and I knew there was no better lunch than the one she would be preparing.

Mum was excited and commenting to my dad about what color ribbon would be on her box, to assure he would be having lunch with her. I was sitting in a chair as Mum brushed my hair. She was about to add the red bow in my hair when I spoke up, saying, 'Don't forget to pack enough for me Mum.'

'Ruby you're old enough to participate this year, so I packed two boxes, one for me and one for you. I will add the same ribbon to the lunch box as I'm putting in your hair, and then it's easy for everyone to know what box yours is.'

I'm sure my mouth fell open. I tried to remain calm, but I couldn't speak, or even formulate words. My face grew hot and as red as that stupid bow in my hair. Something was rising inside me as the banter between Mum and Dad continued. Finally, I couldn't contain it any longer. I blew my top! I jumped up out of the chair, ripped the ridiculous red bow from my hair and in a loud voice said, 'I'm not a BOX SOCIAL. I'm not a lunch that you can decorate! I HATE IT! I HATE THE WHOLE IDEA OF IT! The box social, and this ridiculous bow in my hair.'

I threw the red ribbon on the floor and stomped on it. 'I hate this bow; I'm never wearing it again.'

Mum didn't know what to think and it took her a minute to formulate a response. Then with a soft voice she said, 'Ruby, I have never seen you so angry.'

## Nancy

Anger is a natural reaction experienced by all humans at one time or another and can occur for several reasons:

Anger historically has been a function for survival. A natural response to danger or a threat causing the brain to release adrenaline and activating a fight, flight, freeze or fawn response to keep us safe from the danger.

Anger can also develop out of frustration, the feeling of powerlessness or lack of control.

Anger can be a response to an injustice that has happened to oneself or a loved one at the hands of another person.

Anger can occur out of frustration over an expected outcome versus an actual outcome where the reality is opposite to what was expected.

Anger can occur when someone does not respect boundaries.

The above are all antecedents to anger, and regardless of what causes the anger to occur, the common denominator is our brain detecting a threat. This threat can be real or simply perceived.

The behaviours associated with anger are designed to warn

an aggressor to stop their threatening behaviour.

There are three phases of anger:

A preparation phase when the body prepares for battle after a threat has been detected. There is an increase in heart rate and blood pressure. Muscles tense and the voice is altered, often becoming louder, pupils enlarge, rapid breathing occurs and the skin, especially in face and neck, becomes flushed.

An action phase when an individual responds to the threat. This phase is when anger is externalized verbally and/or physically. One may use hateful words, scream, bang their fists, slam doors, or stomp their feet.

The reflection phase occurs after the action phase and is when the individual is reflecting on their own behaviour, the outcome, and consequences. If there was an out of character outburst, aggressive fist banging or violence, the individual may feel shame and regret.

Today there are psychoeducational interventions and programs called anger management in which information is provided to its participants about anger, encouraging awareness of responses when individuals become angry. These anger management programs are designed to normalize anger while also helping participants recognize what behaviours are displayed during the action phase; behaviours that may not be helpful, and some behaviours that may even be abusive. We hear a lot about road rage today. A phenomenon where an individual feels threatened or wronged when cut off in traffic and perceives this as a personal assault or intentional wrongdoing on the other driver's part. In these road rage cases the driver thinks or believes something that may or may not be true. The other driver may simply be a bad driver, or a careless driver, with no mean intention at all. Programs like anger management help people to ponder different perspectives and reframe situations while also facilitating alternative responses to these situations.

Anger management is not about stopping the anger but teaching about anger, drawing awareness to anger, promoting the understanding of anger and normalizing anger while planning for alternative behaviours during the action phase to reduce the likelihood of shame and regret.

Anger can have many beneficial outcomes. Anger can help set boundaries when people are in our space or taking too much from us. Anger can also cover up emotions we are not comfortable with such as vulnerability. Anger can also act like an armour keeping people away, giving us space and protecting us when we feel unsafe. Anger can help us to get what we want and may be a cue that an injustice is happening, and we need to speak up or act accordingly. Anger can be a venue for expressing emotions, facilitating change, and resolve problems. Anger itself is normal and has purpose. Anger becomes a problem when we don't understand it, don't allow it, or don't know how to respond to it appropriately.

The trick with anger is to notice it when its small and act or speak before it grows into a larger issue, causing one to feel out of control. As humans we sometimes get mixed up and think we can absorb small amounts of anger and choose not to do anything so no one would ever know that one was ever angry. This is not sustainable, as anger needs to be processed. What happens is after so many meals of anger one will blow their top, and be out of control, not even being able to think straight. If one can speak up when an injustice or frustration occurs the first time, there is a stronger probability for problem solving and processing of anger.

A belief that anger is a bad thing can be damaging to the body. The rush of adrenaline received during the preparation phase promotes action to solve the problem or issue at hand. When anger is not given the opportunity to be processed, adrenaline lives within the body and has detrimental effects.

Society has historically accepted anger in men and normalized violent behaviours displayed during the action phase of anger. Anger has been discouraged in females with messages of anger being wrong and not lady like. It is not accepted within society for a woman to be angry. These messages to young females can cause girls to internalize their anger and deny its existence.

Unprocessed anger can lead to physiological illness such as heart disease, inflammation, and chronic fatigue. It can increase Incidents of road rage, initiate partner violence, and assaults.

We are hearing about an increase in drivers having altercations with other drivers resulting in fist fights and violence breaking out on highways and roads. I have a simple theory as to why this is happening:

1. Internalized unprocessed anger has been occurring and may be bubbling right at the surface. It won't take much to reach the boiling point, so when a driver cuts them off, they BLOW THEIR TOP.

2. They are not aware of other options they have during

the action phase and may have seen violent role models responding to anger with violence and aggression. The result is a learned response to the emotion of anger, or possibly the feeling of vulnerability.

Oh, by the way, after my mom expressed her anger over the box social and distaste of the ribbon in her hair, my grandmother never added that finishing touch again, and my mom was happy about that.

Brian Scott McCoy is a practicing attorney who wrote his first book called *The Box Social*. It is based on a true story set in a small town in the early 1900s and tells of young love and simpler times, courtship and what fate has in store at the box social.

# Dear Diary

*Ruby*

Dear Diary: You will not believe what happened today. I am ugly with myself and disappointed. You see I received a 9.5 out of 10 on a test. I studied hard. I knew all the answers. Before passing it in, I double checked, and I was certain that all my answers were correct. One of the questions was, who was the author of *The Ugly Duckling*? I knew the answer and wrote extra so my teacher would know how hard I studied. My answer was thorough. *The author of The Ugly Duckling was Hans Christian Anderson, a Danish author who was born in 1805, and died in 1875. The book* The Ugly Duckling *was written in 1843.* I will get extra points for that one I thought! The teacher however did not give me extra points, and in fact took points away. I couldn't believe it. What I learned though is the spelling of the author's name.  His last name is not spelled A-N-D-E-R-S-O-N, but A-N-D-E-R-S-E-N. I didn't realize this until today. I guess this was a learning experience, and I will never forget the spelling. Realizing this now as I write this all down in my diary.

I love writing in this diary. I love the little lock so I can be assured no one sees my private thoughts. Aunt Sadie knows I love books and knew I would love this diary when she and Uncle Louis gave it to me for Christmas last year. I can look back and see how different my circumstances were a few months ago. In April I had a crush on Burpee Wagner. He's a leader in our one room schoolhouse - outspoken, smart, and his mom loves to quilt and host quilting bees. Burps' dad is known for picking strawberries and has a great sense of humour. Today though I realized something. I respect Burpee and his leadership qualities. I admire him but no longer have a crush on him. There's another boy I have my eye on now named Harold. I keep these thoughts to myself though, I don't want anyone to think I'm boy crazy, I want everyone to think of me as smart like Burpee Wagner, a good student who loves books, studying hard and helping the teacher out when she needs an assistant.

## Nancy

Not as many people today still use pen and paper diaries, as there is more focus on social media, blogs, and creating TikTok videos. Writing in a diary has tremendous mental health value. There are several benefits for having a diary. It improves writing skills. The more we engage in something, the better we become at it, so the more we write the better writers we become.

Writing is a simple and effective tool for the promotion of well-being and good mental health. It allows the writer to pause and reflect on their thoughts, feelings, opinions, and circumstances while providing a space for creativity and self-expression.

Journaling is a therapeutic intervention and is widely used as a form of treatment for mental illness and as a prevention tool to promote good mental health. It is a mindful activity that holds our attention to the present with pen and paper. When writing thoughts and feeling out on paper it increases the probability of finding solutions and insights. It can also help keep thoughts organized. Recording daily feelings, emotions, thoughts, and opinions strengthens the ability to understand and make sense of our lives.

Writing helps set goals and a diary can be a place to write ambitions and aspirations. Recording goals can monitor progress and motivate the writer to achieve goals and celebrate new milestones.

Keeping a diary inspires creativity and can be fun. It is a creative outlet allowing expression for those people who struggle to express themselves by talking. It provides a space for self-reflection and self-awareness. Reflecting promotes understanding and insights on patterns of thoughts and behaviours that can promote growth, change and a sense of being in control, and the ability to handle issues and stress in the future.

Articulating emotions, feelings and experiences helps manage and regulate emotions while reducing their intensity. It provides the writer with an avenue for mind mapping and considering both solutions and different perspectives.

Writing promotes positivity and gratitude. Putting into words what one is grateful for each day encourages a positive outlook on life.

Writing in a diary can provide self-awareness on the writer's character, personality, and values, along with what is important and how they want to be seen by others. It's an activity that encourages the writer to be aware of how they are feeling inside and making sense of these feelings. It shapes the writer's connection with themselves, which in turn promotes confidence, motivation, goal setting and perception of events, reducing the likelihood of rumination or obsessive thinking.

Putting pen to paper relieves stress by allowing the brain to 'dump' feelings and emotions onto paper, externalizing those uncomfortable feelings within and making sense of our thoughts and feelings. Today, therapists help their clients by normalizing thoughts and emotions that are appropriate for the situation. Writing in a diary or journal can help an individual normalize their own thoughts and feelings and bring a sense of acceptance and calm, knowing their thoughts and feelings makes sense. Acceptance of what is happening within instead of judging the self, experiences, and circumstances can be helped by journaling.

Writing things down also boosts memory. The brain stores information better when it is written down, and we have better recall after writing things down. Have you ever noticed that when you write out a grocery list you tend to remember what's on the list once you get to the store? If you don't write it down do you forget essential items? This is an example of the brain storing information and promoting better recall once we write out a list.

Diaries come in all shapes and sizes. I prefer the ones that lock with a key, even better is a combination code which minimizes the risk of losing the key, or someone else finding the key. I prefer a diary that has a leather cover with that vintage smell of leather. There are lots to choose from. So, if you are buying one, choose one that speaks to you. A lock or combination will ensure no one finds your diary of private thoughts and reads it by 'accident'. You wouldn't want anyone to know who your secret crush is.

Oh, by the way, my mom, Ruby was right about Burpee Wagner. He became the mayor of a town in New Brunswick and held this position for 20 years. A leader indeed.

# Phobias

Ruby

My second cousin once removed was named Ralph Floyd. He moved back to the Meadow Road in Titusville after a long hiatus from the community of over 20 years. His family home had sat empty for years and needed repair, so I wasn't sure how Ralph was managing. Ralph was in his forties, never married, and worked many years for the circus, carnivals, and exhibitions. He travelled all over with the circus as it went from town to town.

At school, I told my friend and classmate Harold about Ralph, and invited him to join me after school to pay Ralph a visit. Mum was sending some pickles with me to give to Ralph as a welcome home gift. I told Harold that Ralph was a colorful chap that loved animals. Harold said he had a cousin that sounded very similar to Ralph that lived alone in Maine, and his family referred to him as the hermit of Moosehead Lake. Harold was happy to accompany me and to meet Ralph. When school ended, we made our way over to Meadow Road, took a short cut through the cemetery and up Ralph's long driveway.

There were four or five geese waddling towards us. One gander was quite aggressive, flapping his wings and honking at us. Harold laughed and shooed the geese away; he was used to geese and thought their behaviour was humorous. As we approached the door of Ralph's house, we could see that some windows did not have any glass and the front door was wide open. Bushes, hay, and grass were overgrown around the property. We spotted a goat on the roof of a small shed and another grazing on a flowering bush underneath an apple tree close to the shed. Harold joked that the goat likely climbed the apple tree to get on the roof.

I was beginning to regret bringing Harold here as we entered the back porch and a pack of dogs ran up to us, jumping all over us before making their way outside. We could hear the barking and the geese honking as we called for Ralph. Harold was wiping the dog hair from his pants, a smile still on his face, which put my mind more at ease. We entered what I think was the parlour. It was hard to tell as there were vines that had grown in through the windows and up the walls. There was a large pig laying on a sofa snoring, and Ralph was in a chair sound asleep with a monkey dressed in a red striped sweater on top of him. The monkey immediately spotted us, hurried to Harold, climbed up onto his shoulder, and began inspecting his hair. Harold thought this too was hilarious. The floor in the house was a dirt floor, and it was difficult to tell at times that we were indoors; it felt a bit more like being in a barn with furniture.

Ralph awoke with a startle, shooed the pig off the sofa and pushed it towards the open front door. The pig reluctantly went outside grunting and swishing its tail through the front entryway. Ralph invited us to sit down where the pig had been sleeping. I chose to stand and gave Ralph the pickles Mum had sent with me. Harold sat on the couch where the pig had been sleeping, although he had to lean forward as there were so many thick vines growing on the walls behind his head. Ralph was happy to receive the gift and expressed his gratitude with a giant grin that exposed only one tooth. Ralph had long hair down his back and wore a bright yellow sweater with a hole in it. He was very friendly, and after a few minutes of small talk he went into the next room and came back with a small ALLIGATOR! Ralph told us of his adventures with the circus and all the animals that he tended to and collected. The typical pets such as dogs, geese and goats, and the not so typical pets: a monkey, a pig, an alligator, and a few snakes. I noticed Harold's demeanor was changing; he looked as white as a ghost and his smile was gone. Ralph looked behind Harold and announced his snakes were friendly, not real big, and were harmless. Harold now had sweat forming on his brow. 'They like to stay in those vines behind you Harold, they will show themselves eventually.' The words were barely out of Ralphs mouth when Harold shot up off the sofa and ran out of the house faster than a streak of lightning. It was this day that I learned more about my eccentric cousin Ralph, and that my friend Harold had a phobia of snakes.

## Nancy

A phobia is an uncontrolled and irrational fear of something that poses no actual threat or danger. A phobia is a type of anxiety disorder where symptoms only appear when around the source of the phobia, although sometimes even the thought of the phobia source can cause feelings of panic.

There are different types of phobias. Animal phobia is a fear of animals such as dogs, spiders, snakes, or rodents. Situational phobias involve a situation or event such as flying or going to the dentist which causes fear. Environmental phobias include fear of heights, dark water, or small spaces. Some phobias involve the body such as fear of blood or vomit. Usually, these types of phobias are simple phobias and can be managed, not interrupting one's daily routines or functioning. Symptoms of simple phobias only occur when the source of phobia is in proximity.

Complex phobias are a different story, and can be debilitating, interrupting routine and daily functioning. Agoraphobia (fear of large spaces) and social phobia (fear of a lot of people) are examples of complex phobias. These types of phobias can cause isolation and lack of connection as they can keep one from leaving their home.

Even though the person with a phobia knows their fear is irrational, they are still unable to control their reaction and they typically manage their fear by keeping away from places where the source of phobia may exist. A fear of dogs will lead to avoidance of parks or trails frequented by dogs. The anxiety symptoms become worse the closer proximity to the phobia source, so the closer a dog gets, the more anxious/panicked the individual will feel.

The amygdala is a part of the brain that's role is to detect danger. The amygdala is constantly scanning the environment looking for danger, and when a threat is detected the brain releases stress hormones and adrenaline throughout the body so one can either escape or fight the danger. This is called the fight or flight response. This response when danger is detected keeps us safe, giving added adrenaline to our muscles and a boost of energy to get us away from the threat. This response is an instinctual response to a threat, and the amygdala's job is to detect any danger, and send essential messages to the rest of our body to prepare us to RUN or FIGHT.

With phobias, the amygdala is detecting danger around the phobia source - even though there is no real danger, the amygdala senses there is. People with phobias do not choose this fear. It is not attention seeking nor is it in their control. Those who have a specific phobia know there is no real threat but cannot control their reaction to the issue or object that is the phobia source.

Anxiety symptoms during an encounter may include light-headedness, dizziness, a pounding heart, sweating, shortness of breath, shaking and tingling sensations usually accompanied by the feeling of being trapped, in danger and a need to escape the situation. These physical sensations are all the outcome of the amygdala sensing danger and preparing the body to get away from the danger, even though there is no real threat.

Why do some people have phobias while others do not? It's not known exactly; however, it is suspected that phobias may stem from the following:

1. Phobias may develop after a stressful or traumatic event that an individual has suffered. For example, a fear of dogs may develop after being attacked by a dog.

2. A phobia may be a learned response that develops at an early age from watching a parent or relative's response to an item/ animal or situation. A child sees the parent's response to a dog as fear and learns this same response.

3. Genetics. There is a family history of phobias and is passed on through generations.

Most sufferers know logically their fear makes no sense yet cannot stop the panic response from happening. Calming techniques to reduce the duration of panic symptoms after an exposure helps manage the fear. Challenging negative thoughts about the phobia source can help, but phobias are usually not due to irrational thinking patterns, but rather a body response when the amygdala part of the brain has detected danger.

Exposure therapy slowly teaches the brain that there is no danger by first helping the phobia sufferer to calm their body when the fear source is introduced, starting first by looking at a picture of the phobia source.

If there is a trauma history that may be related to the phobia, such as the fear of dogs after a dog attack, therapies like EMDR will desensitize and reprocess the traumatic event so the brain knows that the threat is in the past. After a stressful event the brain may have trouble storing information from the event. The brain may become stuck in flight or fight mode causing the body to startle easy by anything similar to the traumatic event. For example, the response to a dog after a dog attack is heightened, as if every dog is now very dangerous. The amygdala's job is to sense danger and alert the body so it can prepare to escape or fight. The amygdala becomes super focused after a traumatic incident, such as a dog attack. Becoming sensitive to anything similar to the traumatic incident, essentially believing that one dog attacked and therefore all dogs are dangerous. The brain is making an association that because one dog was dangerous all dogs are dangerous. The amygdala is fulfilling its biological role, however in cases like this, its working overtime. Therapies like EMDR help the brain to realize it doesn't need to work overtime by integrating information in an adaptive manner, so instead of the brain being wired as 'ALL dogs are dangerous, I am in danger when they are around', the brain creates new pathways and connections to a more realistic view. The negative or fearful view becomes more adaptive and realistic, turning into a belief such as, 'not all dogs are dangerous; that incident is over and I'm safe now'. EMDR therapy helps the brain and body know the trauma is over and in the past. Therapies such as EMDR and exposure therapy can help reduce and even eliminate the fear associated with phobias.

*School of Fear* is a quirky, fun read for 9–12-year-olds. Written by Gitty Daneshvari, the book tells the story of four main characters, all 12 years old, who have phobias that go to a summer school to help them overcome their fears. It is a fictional, whimsical tale on curing phobias. A great read for any age if you enjoy fantasy and villains.

Oh, by the way, I picked this book as the main characters would have been around the same age as my mom, Ruby and dad, Harold, when they paid a visit to Ralph, who was a quirky character himself. I'm pretty sure Dad's fear was passed down from my grandmother, his mother, who also feared snakes, and in turn Dad passed it along to me.

*Ralph Floyd's house*

# Depression

This story is not from the 1940s but rather from 1973. A story about my grandfather Floyd, Ruby's father.

My grandfather lived in the sweetest little house beside my Uncle Gordon's store. During the day, Grampy would sit at the store and 'get all the news' from the patrons of the store.

The floors in Grampy's little house were waxed and shiny. His Christmas decorations were out of this world and up before Labour Day weekend in September. He had beautiful petunias in his garden, and greeted me with a smile, excitement, and a hug every visit. I never knew my grandmother, Mae, as she died before I was born. He and Grammy had a plan to retire from farming and focus on rest and relaxation after many years of hard work on the farm and raising their five children. What wasn't part of the plan was my grammy getting cancer and dying just months after retiring from the farm and moving into their little retirement home. Grampy would continue to keep a spotless house, as Mae would have wanted, and he continued to have beautiful flower gardens as Mae would have also wanted. He welcomed everyone into his home as Mae would have wanted. Grampy knew everyone in Titusville, and everyone knew him. One day in 1973 everything changed. There had been a terrible accident. Ruby explained to me that Grampy was cleaning his gun after hunting season. When he was cleaning his gun, he forgot to check if the gun was loaded, and during the cleaning process the gun went off by accident, the bullet hitting his face.

Grampy was still alive but in the hospital in serious condition. Mom was at the hospital around the clock and talked to him even though he was not conscious. She told him over and over, 'Please Dad, don't leave us, who will fix Nancy's toys?' Please Dad you need to fix Nancy's toys, come back to us, Dad. Nancy needs you.'

Nothing short of a miracle happened next. My grandfather woke up, and after several reconstructive surgeries was able to go home. The bullet had taken off the entire side of his face, entering under his chin taking off his jaw, his teeth, his cheek bone on one side, and one eye. The bullet then exited through his temple. He would never again eat solid foods, nor be able to speak properly. He was amazing in how he dealt with it, wearing sunglasses, and buying a special appliance so he could puree his food. He continued to sit at the store and talk to everyone, he continued to keep a spotless house, and continued to put up Christmas decorations way too early and continued to be excited whenever I would visit. My mother would say he was in a terrible hunting accident, and we all carried on.

When I was thirteen, I learned from the neighbourhood kids that my grandfather was not in a hunting accident, nor was he cleaning his gun when it fired. My grandfather attempted to take his own life. When I confronted my mother with this new information, she didn't argue, but advised me not to talk about it anymore with anyone. It was something that should not be discussed.

My grandfather attempted suicide. The grief of losing his wife so young combined with the grief of losing the retirement they had planned became too much, and depression took over his life. In the 1970s no one talked about emotions or feelings. It would be shameful if a person or family was not seen as perfect. Depression was not even a well-known word in 1973. Mental illness in those days translated to '*You're crazy*', so of course no one talked about their private thoughts and feelings. Mental illness wasn't understood, and considered shameful with connotations one was flawed, maybe even dangerous, and needed to be locked up, so of course no one discussed it.

Ignoring the symptoms of depression and hiding these symptoms fosters shame and make depression worse.

Depression is a mood disorder that causes persistent feelings of sadness. Depression can happen to anyone, however those who have lived through abuse, a severe loss or a stressful event are more likely to develop depression. The risk of depression also increases with age.

Along with severe prolonged sadness, other symptoms may also include excessive guilt, low self-worth, and feelings of hopelessness which can lead to suicidal thoughts and attempts. The pain of depression can lead people suffering to view death as a relief.

Today we are more informed about depression; we know what it is, and medical doctors know how to diagnose, and treat depression. There are several types of medications that treat depression, and often psychotherapy is recommended. Psychotherapy offers a safe space to talk about feelings with a professional who can reframe the way individuals think, help reframe thoughts, and facilitate awareness on what the patient is feeling while offering support. Sometime awareness alone can bring people relief. Knowing what's going on within them and that they are not alone can restore hope and lessen the burden and pain that depression causes.

Today we know that there are many types of depression which include the following:

1. Complicated grief - this occurs when the feelings of loss are debilitating and do not improve over time. This type of grief may turn into depression and lead to suicide.
2. Situational depression - when symptoms of depression occur after a stressful or traumatic event. The depression is a reaction to the stressful event.
3. Depression that is accompanied by anxiety, so there are symptoms of both anxiety and depression.
4. Seasonal affective disorder - a type of depression that occurs during certain seasons of the year, usually in fall and winter when days are shorter and there is less daylight.

Historically it's been believed that depression impacts more women than men, however Terrence Real, a psychotherapist in Newton, Massachusetts, believes this has been a cover up for many years to suggest that depression is not a manly affliction. In his book, *I Don't Want to Talk About It: Overcoming the Secret Legacy of Male Depression* he discusses how men typically hide their condition from friends, family, and themselves to avoid this stigma of being un-manly. Real's book reveals how men can unearth their pain, heal, and find hope again.

With awareness, education and knowledge comes understanding, support, prevention, and treatment.

If you think you may be struggling with depression, or any

other mental illness, please speak to your medical doctor. If you are in crisis there are hotlines available in most cities 24 hours a day. In New Brunswick there is the Chimo help line with staff ready to listen, provide support and offer resources. 1 800 667 5005. In Canada there is a national suicide crisis hot line reachable by dialing 988. Responders are available around the clock to listen and provide support.

*Me (Nancy) and my Grandfather Floyd 1970*

*My grandfather Floyd, me (Nancy) and my cousin Dave in 1982*

# Bill Titus

*by*
*Pat McMullon*

Nancy and I bought our first home in Titusville in 1997. My mother-in-law Ruby was delighted, and eager to introduce me to everyone in the area. I became fast friends with many people in Titusville and found myself on the board of the Titus Hill Cemetery Foundation. I would drive Ruby to meetings, and even spoke at the Baptist Church the Salina Kirk in Salt Springs. Being brought up Catholic and even an altar boy in the Catholic church, this was a big deal for me, however it seemed like the most natural thing to do after Ruby's request to speak. Ruby would often give me a pat on the back and say, 'this is MY son in law,' announcing it like I was something special when she introduced me to people.

J. William (Bill) Titus was a lifelong friend of my mother-in-law, and soon after moving to Titusville, Bill and I became close friends. I would visit his farm and he would tell me stories of yesteryear. Sometimes Bill would drop by our house and Nancy would be quick to offer him a meal or plate of biscuits. It may seem odd to say Ruby and Bill were close friends as Bill and his family lived out West, however, they returned to Titusville when Ruby was a teenager. The Titus family homestead was just down the road from Ruby's house, and she remembered her mother telling her about them. Ruby told me that she remembered waking late one night to look out her window and seeing Billy and his family returning from out West, travelling by train to Hampton and then on home to Titusville, as the road to their farm passed through her family's dooryard in those days. They shared a love of genealogy and beyond that, the stories of the people. Genealogy was always much more than names and dates to Ruby and to Bill. They spent countless hours working to keep the Titus Hill Cemetery vibrant.

A highlight of the year was always the annual Titus Hill Cemetery Service. People would come from near and far every July to see friends and family and remember family members buried in the cemetery. The service consisted of hymns, Bible readings and messages from local clergy. Everyone hoped the weather would co-operate and the service could be held at the cemetery, but inclement weather would sometimes result in the service being held at the Salina Kirk United Church in Salt Springs (near the Burnt Corner, as Ruby used to call it).

I clearly remember a story and message Bill told the assembled crowd one lovely July afternoon, the sun shining down and the ground flox blooming with its beautiful pink flowers. Here is Bill's story and message, to the best of my recollection. I'm not doing it justice, I'm sure, but I can see and hear him telling it on a sunny July afternoon in my mind. A story of angels....

*A group of local hired hands had gathered at the Donnelley farm on the Back River Road in Barnesville one cold Saturday evening in February. Stories were told and some drinks were shared. A fellow named Jim had enjoyed a few extra drinks that night, and as the evening drew late, he announced that he was heading for home. Jim worked and lived at the*

*Titus farm. He could follow the road from Cusack's Bridge, along Green Lake Road and cross the covered bridge in Titusville to get home, but he told his companions that he would instead cut through the Cusack's farm, go through the Titus interval, and cross the Salt Springs Brook instead. A shortcut for sure, but it required wading through the snow and crossing the frozen brook.*

*His friends remained and continued with their evening, but before long, their conversation turned to concern for Jim. He had had too much to drink, and it was a very cold night. They soon agreed that it would be a good idea to follow Jim and make sure he got safely home. So off they set into the clear, cold night. It was a full moon and they quickly caught up to Jim, who was moving more slowly. They decided to keep back and not let him know they were there, just following far enough behind so that he wouldn't notice them. Jim trudged on through the snow and eventually came to the ford on the Salt Springs Brook. The brook was frozen, and Jim stepped out onto the ice. His decision-making was off though, and he fell through the ice when part-way across the brook, sinking into the cold water above his waist. His friends hurried to his aid, fishing him out of the water and getting him safely to the other side. It was only a short distance from the brook to the house and they helped him the rest of the way home, a new story having been born that would be retold for years to come.*

*We sometimes talk of angels and how they appear to help and guide us in our times of need. There are many such stories in the Bible, like when the angels appeared to the shepherds at the birth of Jesus, or when they protected Daniel in the lion's den. I think there are also more subtle ways that angels come into our lives. Perhaps they came through the consciousness of Jim's friends that night and helped turn their thoughts to concern for their friend, leading them to be there when Jim needed them most.*

I'm not sure that it was angels that helped Jim's friends decide to follow him that night or was simply the act of friends thinking about and looking out for one another, but it does give us the opportunity to reflect on the power of friendship and community more broadly. To me, Bill's story is about the importance of looking after and caring for people, whether your friends, like in the story, or beyond. Bill's story reinforces the importance of what can be a small act – yes, Jim's friends ended up pulling him out of the brook, but it was the act of caring, and making sure he got home safely that let that happen.

Maybe I hope that it was angels that helped Jim's friends make their decision. That might show that the greatest way to make an impact on our world is through small, everyday kindness, for the angels chose to guide the actions of Jim's friends rather than just swooping in to pull him from the brook themselves. Maybe the real power, the real miracles, lay in our small, everyday actions.

I spent many hours sitting in Bill's kitchen, discussing almost every imaginable subject. He was wise, welcoming, kind, and he was my friend.

*Nancy*

Billy's house still stands on Meadow Road, past the Titus Hill Cemetery, by the Salt Springs Brook. Billy was a bachelor who was great friends with my mother. A resident of the area recently told me that Billy never married because he was forever in love with Ruby. I'm not convinced this is true, but in 2009 my parent's camp along the Hammond River in Barnesville burnt down. It burnt to the ground with only a heap of ashes remaining. My mother walked through the ash weeks later with a stick, turning over the blackened remnants, hoping to recover something, anything really. She poked at one mound of ashes, the heap separated and revealed a perfect, untouched photograph of Billy Titus.

*Billy Titus*

*Billy's house in Titusville*

*Billy at our son Jack's baptism.*

I hope these stories brought you as much pleasure as I had hearing my mother tell them over the years. Ruby loved genealogy, but much more than just names and dates, she loved the stories of her ancestors, family, and neighbours for how they brought history to life and helped us see that they were real people, just like you and me.

And just like all people throughout history, the people in Ruby's stories have their joys and struggles and manage through them to the best of their abilities. There was a lot of value in the strength of family and community that helped people through hard times, but there were also areas where those traditions came up short. I hope tying in a mental health background to components of these stories can help us all tie our traditions and modern learning together in a way that forges a new and strengthened path forward.

*Photo credit to John Elliott*

*Photo credit to Tammy Smith*

# Bibliography

Glasser ,William. *Choice Theory: A New Psychology of Personal Freedom*. New York: Harper Collins Publishers Inc. 1999

Olver, Kim. *Secrets of Happy Couples*. Chicago: InsideOut Press. 2011

Van der Kolk, Bessel. *The Body Keeps the Score*. New York: Penguin Group. 2014

Shapiro, Francine. *Eye Movement Desensitization and Reprocessing Basic Principles, Protocols and Procedures*. New York: The Guilford Press. 2001

Levine, Peter. *Waking the Tiger*. Berkeley CA: North Atlantic Books. 1997

Gardner, Howard. *Multiple Intelligences New Horizons*. New York: Basic Books. 2006

Nerenberg, Jenara. *Divergent Mind-Thriving in a World That Wasn't Designed for You*. New York: Harper Collins. 2021

Parks Canada. (http://www.parks.canada.ca/docs/v-g/ie/at-ag/agir-action/)

Plant you (http://www.plantyou.com/switchel-recipe/)

Almanac (http://www.almanac.com/switchel-recipe-haymakers-punch)

Wikepedia (http://www.wikepedia.org/wiki/Canada-jay)

Anxiety Canada (http://www.anxietycanada.com/disorders/hoarding-disorder/)

WildLife Trusts (http://www.wildlifetrusts.org/wildlife-explorer/ferns-and-horsetails/addres-tongue-fern)

Better Help (http://www.betterhelp.com/advice/anger/are-there-different-levels-of-anger/)

Help Guide (http://www.helpguide.org/articles/grief/helping-someone-who-is-grieving.htm)

American Academy of Family Physicians (http://www.aafp.org)

The Medical University of South Carolina (http://www.muschealth.org)

Psychology Today (http://www.psychologytoday.com/ca/conditions/hoarding-disorder)

Wallace, Jennifer Breheny. Washington Post (http://washingtonpost.com/national/health-science). 2017

Prevention (http://prevention.com/health/mental-health/g19876574/narcissistic-personality-disorder-symptoms/)